D1543981

Thai
COOKING CLASS

SOMI ANUNTRA MILLER
& PATRICIA LAKE

MURDOCH BOOKS®
Sydney • London • Vancouver • New York

Contents

THAI COOKING

Welcome to the newest edition of 'Thai Cooking Class'. Thai food is food you can enjoy cooking as much as eating with these easy authentic recipes which have made this book a best seller.
Wonderful tastes can be created in your own kitchen with utensils you already have and a minimum of fuss.

Most of the recipes in this book are simple and take less than half an hour to cook. They are traditional recipes, prepared with Western cooks in mind. We tell you where to find the ingredients easily, how to prepare and cook the food correctly and how to use substitutes.

Thai food combines the best of several Eastern cuisines: the oriental bite of Szechwan Chinese, the tropical flavour of Malaysian, the creamy coconut sauces of Southern Indian and the aromatic spices of Arabian food.

Thais then add an abundance of fresh ingredients, coriander plants, chillies and pepper. The result is like a 'cuisine minceur' of the Orient, with small portions of lean meat, poultry and seafood, and plenty of fresh vegetables and salads.

Thai food is lightly cooked so it's crisp, colourful, sharply flavoured and nutritious. The distinctive taste comes from a handful of fundamental ingredients, all widely available at Asian foodstores and delicatessens:

- fresh coriander, including the roots;
- fresh basil, mint and lemon grass;
- garlic, chillies, pepper, onion and shallots;
- coconut milk;
- shrimp paste and fish sauce;
- citrus leaves, especially Kaffir lime leaves; and
- occasionally, dried spices.

Like the word 'Thai' (which means 'free'), Thai cooks are never rigid in their approach. So be flexible in your interpretation of the recipes, particularly if you're not always able to find every ingredient. If you embrace their style and imagination, you'll find your venture into Thai cooking an extremely pleasurable and rewarding one.

It can be economical, too, if you adapt recipes to take advantage of market and seasonal bargains. For instance, Green Sweet Chicken Curry is equally delicious if you use beef, fish or pork instead of chicken.

Good results come with careful planning, quick, vigilant cooking and imaginative presentation. Above all, taste as you cook. Thai is very tasty food and Thai cooks try to strike a balance between sweet, sour, hot, bitter and salty. The cook is meant to enjoy the meal too. Don't hide in the kitchen preparing course after course. Do what the Thais do: put everything on the table at once and get everyone to help themselves.

Save your stir-fried dishes until last and make soups and curries beforehand. Pre-cooked snacks and rice can be heated at the last minute. As long as the rice is steaming, it doesn't matter if the other dishes aren't particularly hot.

Eat with forks and tablespoons (fork in the left hand to push food on to the spoon in the right hand) as they do in Thailand. The Thais do not scoop portions onto their plates as Westerners tend to do (even when eating at Thai restaurants). Instead, they share from common dishes, taking only enough for a bite or two at a time. This way, one avoids seeming too greedy and everyone has an ample share of each dish. Also, it is easier to savour the tastes of a variety of dishes. An important consequence of this eating pattern is that all food must be 'bite-sized'. Thus, proper cutting of ingredients before cooking is an essential part of Thai cuisine.

THE THAI KITCHEN

A walk through a Thai village is like walking through a huge open-air kitchen. Everywhere you look, people seem to be preparing a meal. Everything and everyone is on display. Few houses have built-in or enclosed kitchens. Cooking takes place under a verandah or in a roughly built annexe with mud floors. If there are any walls at all, the windows are wide and unglazed so the smoke and food aromas can waft away.

The stove is a crude charcoal burner, made of either metal or clay, on which sits a wok or large pot. As there are no ovens, you'll find few baked dishes in Thai cuisine. A wooden cupboard is used to store garlic, fish sauce, dried chillies and dried fish. Large earthenware tubs store rainwater, with lids to keep the dust out.

The Thai kitchen may lack gadgets and shiny surfaces, but it is no place of drudgery. Groups of people sit around slicing and chopping, snacking and laughing. The village news and gossip is digested as the next meal is being prepared, and a visitor's offer of help will be rewarded with an invitation to stay for dinner.

Apart from several woks, saucepans and steamers, the most important items in a Thai kitchen are sharp knives and cleavers, some chopping boards, a coconut shredder and a mortar and pestle.

If the Thais are able to improvise with so few utensils, so can we. A wok is a worthwhile investment, but a deep-frying pan will do. A large multi-layered bamboo steamer would be handy, but a cheap fold-out metal one is just as effective, and while it feels good to grind away your frustrations with a mortar and pestle, a food processor, grinder or blender will save a lot of time. If you decide to buy a mortar and pestle, buy one from Thailand. As the mortar is ceramic and the pestle wood, they're specially designed for making moist curry pastes and for bruising lemon grass, citrus rind, garlic and coriander roots. Best of all, they're the cheapest. A Thai mortar

and pestle sells for about the same price as the average wok — the cost of one or two main course dishes at your local Thai restaurant!

While village life in Thailand allows time for daily marketing and traditional making of pastes, stocks and sauces, the urban and middle income Thai families face many of the time restraints we do.

So there is no dishonour in using a food processor instead of a mortar and pestle or any form of shortcut, for that matter, if the end result tastes good. Thai cooks use many shortcuts to make life easier. Ready-made curry pastes, chilli sauces, powdered soup stocks and dried ingredients are commonplace in Bangkok's supermarkets and are widely available in Asian foodstores outside Thailand.

You'll find many ingredients can be frozen and then thawed successfully in a microwave oven. Homemade curry pastes and sauces are worth the effort, but make large quantities and freeze them in measured amounts. Even the roots and stems of coriander and lemon grass can be frozen in plastic wrap. A variety of soup stocks and small individual portions of chicken, beef and pork will always come in handy for quick defrosting in the microwave.

It is important, however, to use fresh herbs, vegetables and seafood wherever possible, and to plan your menus around the best seasonal produce available.

Most stores specialising in Asian groceries outside Asia now have

comprehensive Thai sections, though basics like canned coconut milk, fish sauce, noodles and dried chillies and spices may be cheaper at supermarkets. Some delicatessens and health food stores even stock ingredients like tamarind pulp, powdered galangal and dried lemon grass. If you do have local Asian grocers, get to know them, tell them you're interested in Thai cooking and ask for advice on ingredients. With demand on the increase, more Thai items are becoming available.

If you don't have a local Asian food store, one visit to your nearest city's Chinatown will do — once you have a stock of fundamentals, they'll last a long time.

A word about the cooking routine: always read a recipe from beginning to end before you start. Assemble all the ingredients around you, then prepare. Make sure you have your pre-cut ingredients and pre-measured condiments and spices for each dish handy to the stove. A good idea is to place them in separate little piles on a large plate, one plate for each recipe. That way, you don't get confused if you're cooking several items at once. It's a useful habit to get into and one Thai cooks use.

MEASURING EQUIPMENT

In this book, fresh ingredients are given in grams and ounces so you know how much to buy. A small, inexpensive set of kitchen scales is always handy and very easy to use.

Note that cup and spoon measures are always level.

INGREDIENTS

ASIAN BROCCOLI, CHINESE CABBAGE These are two of the now extensive range of Asian green vegetables available in Chinatowns and larger Asian grocery stores outside Asia. Even larger fruit markets now offer a range of Asian vegetables. European broccoli and cabbage can be substituted but it is worth trying the Asian varieties.

BASIL (BAI HORAPA) There are three types of fresh basil leaves used in Thai cooking. European sweet basil will substitute for all of them. Look for the Thai varieties in Chinatowns in larger cities. Bai Horapa is the nearest to European sweet basil and is readily found in Asian shops. It has a much more pronounced aniseed flavour. Bai Manglak has tiny leaves like dwarf basil and the Thais sprinkle it over salads and soups. Bai Krapao has the strongest flavour. Its leaves are a reddish purple and are used cooked. Basil is available at larger fruit markets and is easy to grow at home.

CHILLI (PRIK) Not all Thai dishes are hot, but chillies are synonymous with Thai cuisine. So much so, it's hard to believe they were only introduced to Thailand after being discovered by Christopher Columbus' expedition to the New World less than 500 years ago. Fresh chillies come in red, green and yellow and in various sizes. Usually the smaller they are, the hotter they taste. Dried chillies are widely available and if necessary can be soaked in hot water for a few minutes before using. Ground chillies, chilli paste or dried chilli flakes can be substituted in some dishes.

To lessen the hotness, use larger chillies and remove the seeds. If you're not used to hot food you can often delete the chilli altogether, and when called for in garnishing, use capsicum (pepper) strips instead. The taste grows on you, however, and you'll be surprised how quickly your tolerance for chilli improves. A warning — take great care when slicing and preparing chillies. Wash your hands and nails thoroughly

after handling them, and keep your hands away from your face and eyes, and from those of children. The oils the chilli skins exude are volatile.

CHILLI PASTE (NAM PRIK PAO) (sometimes called Chilli Paste in Bean Oil, Burnt Mild or Roasted Chilli Paste) This is an ingredient in many Thai recipes, including the famous Tom Yam soups. The paste is made in Thailand and sold in squat jars in the condiments or Thai sections of Asian foodstores. It is made from dried chillies, dried shrimp, roasted onion and garlic, sugar and tamarind juice (see recipe page 29). A small amount of fresh or dried chilli can be used as a substitute.

CHILLI SAUCE (NAM PRIK) There are countless recipes for chilli sauces, to bottle as condiments and to make fresh to accompany noodles and rice, the way Italian sauces accompany spaghetti. Some of the famous Thai bottled sauces, Saus Prik, include 'Sriracha' and 'Sweet Chilli Sauce for Chicken' (it goes with everything, in fact). There are many recipes for homemade traditional spicy hot sauces — no traditional Thai meal would be complete without at least one.

CHINESE FIVE SPICE A brown powdered mixture of star anise, cloves, cinnamon, pepper and fennel, it is used in roast meat and poultry dishes, and is sold in packets or jars in Asian foodstores.

CHINESE GREEN MELON (FAK-KEOW) (sometimes called Bitter Melon, Balsam Pear, Kareala or Bitter Gourd) This is an elongated, wrinkled green fruit sold fresh in Chinatowns. It can also be bought canned in Asian foodstores. Chokos or cucumbers can be substituted.

COCONUT (MAPRAO) AND COCONUT MILK (NAM KATI) Flaked or shredded coconut meat and desiccated coconut are rarely used except for sweets and garnishes. But coconut milk (pulped flesh, not juice) is one of the most important ingredients. It's used in curries, meat, vegetable and seafood dishes as well as for desserts and sweets.

You can make your own by placing 100 g (3½ oz) desiccated (dried) coconut with 300 ml (10 fl oz) hot water in a saucepan and simmering over low heat for about 5 minutes. Strain through a sieve, pushing down on the pulp with the back of a spoon. This will yield roughly 1 cup (250 ml/8 fl oz) of thick coconut milk. A second pressing will give you a thinner milk; just repeat the process using the used coconut and a little less water.

Alternatively, put the warm water and the coconut in a blender, blend for 1 to 2 minutes and sieve. Coconut cream can be skimmed from the top of the milk after it has stood for a few hours in the refrigerator. The easy way out (and sometimes the cheapest) is to buy ready-made, canned coconut milk at major supermarkets. Instant coconut milk powder is now available and is a handy substitute.

CORIANDER (PAK CHEE) (sometimes called Chinese Parsley or Cilantro) Fresh coriander is essential to Thai cuisine. The leaves flavour stir-fried dishes, sauces and curries, and garnish practically everything. The roots and stems are either chopped finely or pounded for marinades and curry pastes. Coriander is now easy to get in larger fruit markets and Asian grocery stores or you can easily grow your own. You can freeze the roots and the first few centimetres (about 1 in) of the stems, wrapped in plastic. When thawed, they're a bit soggy, but they retain their flavour and they really are indispensable. Coriander seeds are sometimes used in curry pastes, too. There is no substitute for the flavour of fresh coriander, but when called for only as a garnish, you can use any fresh herb leaves.

EGGPLANTS/AUBERGINES (MAKEUA POCH) There are many sizes and varieties of eggplant (aubergine) grown in Thailand. They come in white, green, yellow and purple, and taste similar to European kinds. The smallest Thai eggplant (aubergine) is the pea eggplant (makeua puong) which can sometimes be found in Asian foodstores. These little eggplants (aubergines) are used in curries, but if you have difficulty finding this ingredient, you can substitute green peas.

GINGER

GALANGAL

KRACHAI

KAMIN
(FRESH TURMERIC)

TUR POOL
(GREEN BEANS)

WHITE PEPPER

CORIANDER SEEDS

STAR ANISE

CUMIN SEEDS

CINNAMON
STICKS

THAI PARSLEY

BAI HORAPA
(THAI BASIL)

GARLIC CHIVES
AND FLOWERS

LEMON GRASS

MAKEUA POCH
(EGGPLANTS)

FRESH
CORIANDER

WHOA HOM DANG
(THAI SHALLOTS)

CHILLIES

GARLIC

LIMES AND
LIME LEAVES

CURRY LEAVES

DRIED
MUSHROOMS

RED
CURRY PASTE

GREEN
CURRY PASTE

BAI CHAPOU
(ASIAN LETTUCE)

MUSSAMAN
CURRY PASTE

SNAKE BEANS

FISH SAUCE (NAM PLA) Fish sauce is to the Thais what soy sauce is to the Chinese and Japanese. It's a watery, amber-coloured, clear sauce, made from salted and fermented fish. Nam means water and pla means fish. It's rich in protein and B vitamins and its use is widespread. Fish sauce is available in supermarkets and Asian foodstores, is inexpensive and lasts, out of the refrigerator, indefinitely. Thai or Chinese brands are acceptable.

GALANGAL (KAH) (also called Laos in Indonesia, Galangale (Old English), or Siamese Ginger) A member of the ginger family, galangal is a pale yellow root with pink knobs and sprouts. It's sold as fresh or dried pieces in Asian foodstores, or powdered, in health stores. One teaspoon of powder equals roughly a 0.5 cm (¼ in) slice. If you need to slice dried galangal pieces, soak them in hot water for at least 10 minutes. Thais believe galangal has medicinal digestive qualities as well as being a fragrant spice. Fresh galangal needs to be washed well before using. Freeze it or keep it in the crisper of the refrigerator in a plastic bag to prevent it drying out. Our fresh green ginger root is not a substitute.

GARLIC (GRATEUM) Thai garlic is smaller and more tender than ours and is not peeled before use. Pickled garlic is a common snack and ingredient in many noodle dishes and in Thailand is pickled in whole knobs.

European garlic should be peeled unless it's very young and tender. Chopped fried garlic (grateum jeow) can be purchased in stores and is delicious in Thai soups and noodle dishes.

HOISIN SAUCE A sweet, spicy, reddish brown sauce from Chinese cuisine, it is made from soy beans and is usually sold in cans or bottles. Used to marinate roast meats or poultry in Chinese cooking, it can also be combined with other sauces as a dip and is an ingredient in some Thai dishes.

KAFFIR LIMES AND LEAVES (MAKRUT) The Kaffir lime is a little-known member of the citrus family. The fruit has a dark, warty, green rind and little juice, but the skin is rich in aromatic oils. The Thais use the lime zest and the leaves (Bai Makrut). Fresh leaves are now easier to find outside Thailand. Ordinary lime zest and young citrus leaves make reasonable substitutes. However, dried Kaffir lime leaves are available at most Asian foodstores and are inexpensive. You do not have to soak them if they are to go into casseroles or any dish which has enough liquid and cooks them longer than a few minutes, which is necessary to revitalise them. But if you want to slice them into shreds, you will need to soak them, preferably in warm water for 5 to 10 minutes to cut them.

LEMON GRASS (TAKRAI) This favourite Thai herb grows in clumps of tall, slim green reeds, and looks a bit like a large freesia without flowers. Use the pale lower part of the stalk which can be chopped finely, or bruise the tougher, greener part of the stem with a pestle, if larger pieces are required. Lemon grass is easy to grow or you can buy it in bunches at Asian vegetable markets.

You can also buy dried lemon grass at Asian grocers, or powdered at health food stores. Fresh is far superior. In an emergency, substitute dried (soaked for ½ hour), or 3 or 4 strips of lemon peel for 1 tablespoon of lemon grass.

LESSER GINGER (KRACHAI) This is available fresh or dried in packets at Asian foodstores. It is sold under the English name of Powdered Rhizome when used as a powder, or simply as Rhizome when it takes the form of dried, slivered roots. It has a mild flavour and recipes will not suffer too much if you delete it.

LIMES (MANAO) Not to be confused with Kaffir limes, the Thais use small, dark green limes for their juice and to garnish salads. If you don't have limes on hand, substitute lemons for juice and lemon wedges for garnishes. When you see limes or lemons at bargain prices, buy and freeze them. They're often called for in Thai cooking and though they're a bit mushy when defrosted, their juice is quite acceptable. They can be thawed in seconds in the microwave. Alternatively, juice them and freeze the juice in ice cube containers.

You can buy pickled limes, or pickled lemons as they're sometimes labelled, at Asian stores. Included in this book is a recipe for pickled lemons, the only drawback being that you have to keep them for 3 months before you can use them.

MUSHROOMS (HED, HED HOM) Thais use two types of mushrooms. Dried Chinese mushrooms (called hed hom) are used in clear soups and some stir-fried dishes. They need to be soaked in warm water for 20 minutes and their stems discarded. Buy dried Chinese mushrooms at Asian stores.

Thai straw mushrooms can be bought in cans or jars at Asian stores. You can substitute canned champignons or fresh button mushrooms if necessary.

NOODLES (MEE) Here are the four most common noodles used in Thailand:

CELLOPHANE NOODLES (WOON SEN) Made from mung bean flour, they're also called bean-thread noodles, bean vermicelli or glass noodles. They're used in soups and some stir-fried dishes and are tough and semi-transparent before cooking. Soak for several minutes in water before using.

RICE VERMICELLI (SEN MEE) Made from rice, they're also called rice sticks or rice noodles. They vary in size from narrow vermicelli to wider, ribbon-shaped noodles about 0.5 cm (¼ in) wide. The larger noodles should be soaked for at least 30 minutes in warm water, the thinner noodles 10 minutes. It's important to drain them well before using. The only time you don't need to soak them is for Sweet and Sour Crisp Fried Thai Noodles. Then, they puff up when fried in hot oil.

EGG NOODLES (BA MEE) Egg and wheat-flour noodles come from China and Thailand. They're nice on their own with a spicy Thai sauce, especially with any of the dipping sauces. They're also used in stir-fry dishes and soups. Available in large supermarkets and Asian stores.

FRESH RICE NOODLES (GWAYTIO) Packaged wet and folded into a block, you'll often see them on the counter or in the refrigerated section at Asian foodstores in Chinatown. Unwrap but don't unravel them. Simply slice them while folded into whatever size you want. Use in soups or stir-fried dishes.

OYSTER SAUCE (NAMMAN HOI)
A Chinese sauce made from oysters. It's thick, brown, rich and salty and should be used sparingly. Oyster sauce is readily available at most supermarkets now, and in Asian stores.

PICKLED SOY BEAN (TAO CHEOW)
(sometimes called Fermented or Salted Soy Beans) This is sold in bottles in Asian foodstores, with a label in English which says Yellow Bean Sauce. Not an essential ingredient, it can be deleted from a recipe without affecting the flavour too much.

PICKLED WHITE RADISH These are dried and salted Chinese white radishes usually found in plastic bags in Asian foodstores. They keep indefinitely. Simply slice a few pieces off when you need some.

RICE (KHAO) (Long-grain Plain and Jasmine, and Sticky Rice) The Thais use two main varieties — long-grain plain or fragrant jasmine rice and sticky or glutinous rice. Long-grain is served with all meals, and is usually steamed or cooked in rice-cookers so it's light and fluffy. The absorption method also works well. Rinse the rice, then place in a saucepan (which has a lid) and cover the top of the rice with about 3 cm (¼ in or one knuckle's length) of water. Boil rapidly until the water is level with the rice and tunnels appear on the surface. Cover with a tight-fitting lid and turn the heat to very low or off. The rice should be cooked after about 10 minutes. Do not remove the lid (apart from a quick check) until you're ready to serve. Before serving, fluff up with a fork or chopstick. You can also cook rice in your microwave and instructions for this are included on page 28.

Sticky or glutinous rice can be bought at Asian foodstores and takes the place of ordinary rice in the north and north-eastern regions of Thailand (although these days plain long and short-grain rice are making inroads in the region). In central Thailand, sticky rice is used mainly in sweets, particularly for the Thai favourite, Mangoes with Sticky Rice. The secret is to rinse the rice several times and soak it for at least 2 hours, then cook it in a steamer.

SALT Most day-to-day meals, stir-fried dishes and salads do not use salt at all. In the traditional cuisine, salt is rarely used as a flavouring, but as a preservative. You may find salt where fish sauce isn't used — in curry pastes and spicy sauces, pickling recipes such as pickled garlic, salted meats and fish where it's used to aid preserving, and in some desserts (but this use of salt is to satisfy Western palates). Many Thais don't bother with salt.

SESAME OIL This oil, extracted from sesame seeds, has a very strong, nutty flavour. It is most often used in Chinese cooking as a flavouring in soups and stir-fried dishes. It is sold in bottles in Asian foodstores and sometimes at larger supermarkets.

SHRIMP, DRIED (DRIED SHRIMP), DRIED PRAWNS (GOONG HENG)
Small salted prawns (shrimps), dried in the sun, that are sold in packets in Asian foodstores and need to be soaked in warm water for about 20 minutes before using. Dry, they're often pounded and added to pastes and salads or used as a garnish for noodle dishes.

SHRIMP PASTE (KAPI) (also called by the Malay name, Blanchan) It's hard to believe that such a strong-smelling pungent paste can enhance the flavour of anything, but this is a vital ingredient in Thai cuisine. It ranges from a syrupy, pink sauce to a hard, brown, compacted slab. It's made from dried prawns (shrimps) and salt, is rich in B vitamins and, together with fish sauce, is a source of protein in Thai diets. The fresh paste available in jars needs refrigeration. The thick dried pastes do not. But they do need airtight containers because their fishy odour is overwhelming. This paste must be stir-fried or roasted in foil before you can eat it. Anchovy paste can be substituted, but shrimp paste is easy to find at Asian stores.

STAR ANISE Star-shaped seed cluster containing shiny brown seeds. Not related to the well-known anise seed, but to the magnolia family. Used extensively in Chinese cooking, it is readily available.

TAMARIND (MAK KAM PIAK)
Tamarind adds an interesting sour or sharp taste to Thai curries and fish dishes in particular, without the tartness of lemons. The tamarind tree is native to Asia and has fern-like leaves and pods with doughy flesh. When ripe, the pod is brown and brittle on the outside but the pulp is juicy. You can buy tamarind pulp in packets at Asian stores and in health stores. You can also buy jars of either tamarind concentrate (strained pulp) or tamarind liquid. The pulp needs to be soaked in warm water and strained to get tamarind juice. The longer it soaks, the stronger the juice. The concentrate requires the addition of water: 1 teaspoon of tamarind needs roughly 2 tablespoons of water, but this varies, so check the label. Lemon, lime or orange juice can be substitutes; so can a mixture of 6 parts vinegar and 1 part sugar.

THAI SHALLOTS, RED AND BROWN (WHOA HOM DANG) Not to be confused with green shallots, or spring onions, Thai shallots are small cloved onions, similar to spring garlic. They are expensive outside Thailand. Brown or white onions (Whoa Hom Yai and Whoa Hom Lek) are an acceptable substitute. Thai shallots are particularly tasty in curry pastes. In this book when we specify shallots in a recipe we mean green shallots (Ton Hom), or the green stems of spring onions.

TURMERIC (KAMIN) Its use in Thai cuisine reflects the Indian influence. Thais use turmeric in curries and sometimes to colour rice. Fresh, it needs to be peeled and pounded before use. Though it can be bought fresh in Thailand, it's hard to find fresh elsewhere. However, you can buy it powdered in supermarkets everywhere. Turmeric is a relative of the ginger and arrowroot families and is a bright, yellowish orange. Traditionally it was used to colour the robes of Thai monks.

WOOD FUNGUS, WOOD MUSHROOMS (HED HUNU) Not an essential ingredient by any means, but its use in several Thai dishes reflects the Chinese influence. You can buy wood fungus at Asian stores and it keeps indefinitely. It looks like dried bits of burnt paper but when soaked in water, turns into a jelly-like brown substance and is a component of some stir-fried dishes. Always soak before using.

STARTERS
AND
SNACKS

It's not customary in Thailand to have starters or an entrée at meal times, but the Thai people are inveterate snackers. At parties or celebrations much of the food served is snack food with wonderful sauces.

There'll be spicy fish cakes, crisp fried vegetables in featherlight batter, minced pork and seafood in pastries, spring rolls, beef balls and satays.

Alongside this array on makeshift tables under pretty lanterns — the bowls of sauces! Some of them, simple sugar and vinegar based ones with sliced chilli, chopped onion and coriander leaves. Others include the pride of the district, the local version of the Thai's favourite spicy hot sauce, 'Nam Prik'.

'Nam Priks' are a bit like sambals and not only make wonderful dips for snacks and raw vegetables but they can transform a bowl of rice or noodles into a tasty meal.

Sweet and Sour Cucumber Relish (page 14), Satay Sauce (page 16), Spicy Deep-fried Fish Cakes (page 12), Prawn (Shrimp) Satay (page 12)

MIXED SATAYS

While not strictly Thai, satays are now eaten in Thailand as often as in Indonesia, where they originated. The Thais have simply added lemon grass, shrimp paste (kapi) and coriander roots to the satay sauce to give it a distinctive Thai flavour.
The word 'satay' has been adopted by the Thais too. Originally the word may have been a corruption of the English word 'steak', though it now applies to the style of cooking meats, or anything else, on skewers. Another popular satay in Thailand is toast. It's quite a favourite dipped in satay sauce for a mid-morning snack. Here are some other, more meaty, recipes.

200 g (6½ oz) each of beef, chicken and pork, cut in 1 x 5 cm (½ x 2 in) strips or thin, single pieces to be threaded on whole
16 bamboo skewers, soaked in water

MARINADE
2 teaspoons ground turmeric
1 tablespoon sugar
pinch salt
1 teaspoon ground coriander
½ teaspoon ground cumin
4 tablespoons vegetable oil
1 tablespoon fish sauce
2 cloves garlic, finely chopped

TO SERVE
lettuce leaves
tomato slices
cucumber slices
fresh coriander sprigs
Satay Sauce (see recipe page 16)
Sweet and Sour Cucumber Relish (see recipe page 14)

1 Thread up to three or four strips of the meat on each skewer. Place in a shallow dish.
2 TO PREPARE MARINADE: Combine turmeric, sugar, salt, coriander, cumin, oil, fish sauce and garlic in a food processor and blend until smooth. Pour over satays and marinate for at least an hour, rotating sticks occasionally.
3 Grill or barbecue over high heat for about 3 minutes each side, turning several times.

4 Arrange on a bed of lettuce leaves with tomato and cucumber slices. Garnish with fresh coriander. Serve with bowls of Satay Sauce and Sweet and Sour Cucumber Relish.

SERVES 4

SPICY DEEP-FRIED FISH CAKES

TOD MAN PLA

1 kg (2 lb) redfish fillets, or similar type fish
4 tablespoons red curry paste, bought or homemade (see recipe page 31)
100 g (3½ oz) green beans, finely sliced into 3 mm (⅛ in) pieces
3 dried lime leaves, soaked for 10 minutes and sliced
2 tablespoons finely chopped fresh coriander leaves and root
1 egg, lightly beaten
2 teaspoons sugar
½ teaspoon salt
400 ml (12½ fl oz) vegetable oil

TO SERVE
fresh coriander sprigs
sliced cucumber
sliced tomato
Sweet and Sour Cucumber Relish (see recipe page 14)

1 Clean and skin fish fillets in cold water. Drain for 30 minutes. Ensure there are no bones. Cut into small pieces.
2 Blend fish and curry paste in a food processor to a light, fine consistency. Combine in a bowl with beans, lime leaves, coriander, beaten egg, sugar and salt. Knead with your hands until the mixture clings together well. (If it's too wet, place uncovered in the refrigerator for 30 minutes to chill and dry a little.)
3 Shape into 4 cm (1¾ in) patties. Deep-fry in a small saucepan or wok, one or two at a time, turning until golden brown.

4 Garnish with coriander sprigs, sliced cucumber and tomato. Serve with a side bowl of Sweet and Sour Cucumber Relish (see recipe page 14).

SERVES 6

PRAWN (SHRIMP) SATAY

GOONG SATAY

MARINADE
1 clove garlic, finely chopped
1 teaspoon ground turmeric
1 coriander root, finely chopped
pinch salt
1 teaspoon sugar
1 tablespoon oil
16 large green prawns (shrimps), peeled, deveined, with tails intact
16 bamboo skewers, soaked in water to avoid charring
Satay Sauce (see recipe page 16), to serve

1 TO PREPARE MARINADE: In a bowl combine chopped garlic, turmeric, coriander root, salt, sugar and oil. Add prawns (shrimps) and ensure they are well covered. Refrigerate for at least 20 minutes.
2 TO PREPARE SKEWERS: Thread prawns (shrimps) onto satay skewers using one prawn per skewer. Grill or barbecue over high heat until pink, about 2 minutes each side. Serve with Satay Sauce.

SERVES 4

Threading prawns (shrimps) Thai style.

Thai Curry Puffs with Sweet and Sour Cucumber Relish and Satay Sauce.

THAI CURRY PUFFS

GURI PAK

FILLING
1 clove garlic, chopped
4 tablespoons vegetable oil
1 onion, sliced
1 tablespoon chopped
coriander root
1 tablespoon ground turmeric
300 g (10 oz) lean pork, chicken
or beef, minced
1 tablespoon sugar
2 teaspoons salt
1 teaspoon pepper, white or black
200 g (6½ oz) cooked
mashed potato
2 tablespoons chopped shallots
(spring onions)

PUFFS
750 g (1½ lb) prepared puff pastry,
slightly thawed
400 ml (13 fl oz) vegetable oil, for
deep-frying

TO SERVE
Sweet and Sour Cucumber Relish
(see recipe page 14)
Satay Sauce (see recipe page 16)

1 TO PREPARE FILLING: In a wok or
frypan, stir-fry garlic in oil until
golden. Add onion, coriander root and
turmeric. Stir-fry several minutes. Add
minced meat, sugar, salt and pepper.
Stir-fry until meat is tender.
2 Lower the heat. Add potato and mix
in well. Taste to see if extra sugar or
pepper is needed. Add shallots, stir
briefly, then remove from heat. Transfer
to a large bowl to cool.

3 Cut one sheet of puff pastry into four
equal squares. Lay one square flat with
a corner towards you. Place about
1 tablespoon of filling in the middle
of the square. Lift the bottom corner
nearest you over to meet its opposite
corner, forming a triangular parcel. Seal
the edges with your fingers, pinching
the pastry to form a curly border, or
using a fork to indent a fancy edge
(see *Note*). Put a twist in each 'wing' of
the pastry, towards the centre then away
again. Set aside on greaseproof paper.
Repeat until all the mixture is used.
4 Deep-fry in vegetable oil in a
saucepan or wok, frying several at a
time until golden brown. Serve with
Sweet and Sour Cucumber Relish and
Satay Sauce.
Note: If you prefer, cut out 10 cm (4 in)
diameter rounds of pastry and brush the
edges with water. Place one tablespoon
of filling on one side. Fold over and
pinch edges together to form 'half
moon' curry puffs.

MAKES ABOUT 20

1 *Cut puff pastry sheet into four equal pieces.*

2 *Take one piece, corner towards you. Place
1 tablespoon mix in centre.*

3 *Fold, pinching to form a curly border. Put a
twist in each wing of pastry.*

Prawn (Shrimp) and Pork Toast. Make them any shape you like, but keep their size uniform so they cook evenly.

PRAWN (SHRIMP) AND PORK TOAST
KANOM PANG MUU GOONG

2 tablespoons finely chopped fresh coriander roots
2 cloves garlic, finely chopped
300 g (10 oz) prawns (shrimps), finely chopped
250 g (8 oz) minced pork
2 onions, finely chopped
3 tablespoons finely chopped green shallots (spring onions)
1 egg, lightly beaten
1 teaspoon white pepper
1 tablespoon fish sauce
10 slices stale bread, crusts trimmed
400 ml (13 fl oz) vegetable oil
fresh coriander sprigs, to garnish

1 Pound coriander root and garlic together to make a paste. Combine in a mixing bowl with prawns (shrimps), minced pork, onions, shallots, beaten egg, pepper and fish sauce. Knead mixture thoroughly until it clings together well.
2 Spread evenly to a thickness of 1 cm (½ in) over bread, making sure it covers the edges. Cut into the shapes of your choice, eg squares or triangles or use fancy pastry cutters if you like.
3 Deep-fry several at a time in vegetable oil, meat-side down first. Fry 1 to 2 minutes until golden then turn over and fry the other side. When golden all over, remove and drain on absorbent kitchen paper. Keep warm in the oven until ready to serve. Garnish with coriander sprigs. Serve with dipping sauces of your choice.

SERVES 4

SWEET AND SOUR CUCUMBER RELISH
THANG KWA PREOW WAN

½ cup (125 ml/4 fl oz) vinegar
250 g (8 oz) sugar
1 teaspoon salt
3 tablespoons water
1 small onion, finely diced
1 small carrot, finely chopped
1 green cucumber, finely chopped
fresh coriander leaves, chopped, to garnish

1 Boil vinegar, sugar, salt and water in a saucepan for 1 minute. Mix onion, carrot and cucumber pieces in a serving bowl. Pour vinegar mixture over vegetables until they are just covered.
2 Taste to see if extra vinegar, sugar or salt is needed to balance flavours. For those who prefer a spicy cucumber relish, add a finely sliced chilli or some chilli paste.
3 Garnish with chopped coriander leaves. Serve with satays, fish cakes and crispy deep-fried snacks.

MAKES ABOUT 350 ML (11½ FL OZ)

SAVOURY SEAFOOD ROLLS

HAE GUEN

2 sheets beancurd skin (see *Note*)

FILLING
**200 g (6½ oz) redfish fillets
or similar, fish bones removed
and flesh chopped**

**200 g (6½ oz) raw or cooked
prawns (shrimps)**

100 g (3½ oz) pork fat, chopped

1 small onion, chopped

6 cloves garlic, chopped

**3 tablespoons chopped fresh
coriander root**

1 tablespoon fish sauce

2 teaspoons sugar

2 teaspoons white pepper

TO SERVE
sliced cucumber

fresh coriander sprigs

**Sweet Chilli Dipping Sauce
(see recipe page 16)**

**Sweet and Sour Cucumber Relish
(see recipe page 14)**

1 Soak beancurd skins in warm water
to soften. Drain well.

2 TO PREPARE FILLING: Combine fish,
prawns (shrimps), pork fat, onion,
garlic, coriander root, fish sauce, sugar
and pepper in a bowl. Marinate for at
least 10 minutes. Process in small
batches in a food processor to achieve a
fine, lightly textured mixture.

3 Take one beancurd sheet. Spoon out
half the mixture in a long, sausage-
shaped mound down the longest edge.
Roll up, sealing edge with water and
pinching both ends. Repeat with
remaining mixture on the other sheet.

4 Steam for 20 minutes or deep-fry in a
large wok for 1 to 2 minutes until
golden. Drain on absorbent kitchen
paper. Leave for at least 45 minutes to
cool and set firmly. Slice diagonally into
2 cm (¾ in) thick slices. Allow 4 to
6 slices per person.

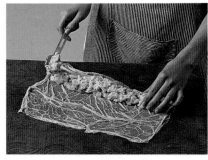

1 *Take one beancurd sheet and spoon out half
the mix in a sausage-shaped mound down the
longest edge.*

2 *Roll up, sealing edges with water and
pinching both ends.*

5 Garnish with cucumber and
coriander sprigs. Accompany with
separate bowls of Sweet Chilli Dipping
Sauce and Sweet and Sour Cucumber
Relish. Serve as an entrée or appetiser
to a Thai feast.

Note: Beancurd sheets or skins are
sometimes called dried tofu sheets, and
are available from Asian food stores.

SERVES 4

3 *Steam for 20 minutes.*

4 *Slice diagonally and serve garnished.*

❖ **SPRING ROLL WRAPPERS**
*Ready made spring roll wrappers are available
fresh or frozen from stores. They can be stored,
wrapped in plastic, in the freezer. Do not leave
the wrappers exposed to air for too long as they
will dry out and become brittle.*

❖ **LEMON GRASS**

Lemon grass is a tall, reed-like plant. The whitish bulb of the grass is used to give a lemon flavour to dishes. While fresh lemon grass is best, it is also available dried and in jars.

SATAY SAUCE

NAM JIM SATAY

1 small onion, chopped
1 tablespoon finely chopped lemon grass
½ teaspoon shrimp paste
3 dried red chillies or 1 teaspoon chilli powder
2 cloves garlic
½ teaspoon ground cumin
½ teaspoon ground coriander
2 coriander roots, chopped
1 cup (250 ml/8 fl oz) coconut milk
1 teaspoon vegetable oil
150 g (5 oz) ground roasted peanuts or crunchy peanut butter
2 tablespoons sugar
2 tablespoons tamarind juice
pinch salt

1 In a blender, combine onion, lemon grass, shrimp paste, chillies, garlic, cumin, coriander and coriander roots with enough coconut milk to moisten.
2 Heat oil in a saucepan. Gently stir-fry onion mixture until it turns a pale pinky brown. Add remaining coconut milk, stirring briskly. Reduce heat to low.
3 Add peanuts and stir well to separate. Then add sugar and tamarind juice and a pinch of salt. If the sauce if too thick, add extra coconut milk. If it's too thin, simmer very gently to reduce — coconut milk and peanuts burn easily.

SERVES 4

SWEET CHILLI DIPPING SAUCE

NAM JIM WAN

100 g (3½ oz) pickled plums (see *Note*)
4 large fresh red chillies
3 cloves garlic
125 g (4 oz) sugar
1 teaspoon salt
½ cup (125 ml/4 fl oz) vinegar
1 teaspoon tamarind juice (optional)
3 tablespoons water
chopped fresh coriander leaves, to garnish

1 Boil pickled plums for several minutes in water. Drain then blend with a little plum juice for a few seconds in a food processor. Pour into a saucepan. Set aside.
2 Roughly blend chillies and garlic. Add to plum purée with sugar, salt and vinegar and tamarind juice, if using.
3 Simmer mixture for about 10 minutes, taking care not to let it burn or stick to the bottom of the saucepan.
4 Taste to see if extra sugar, salt or vinegar is needed. The flavour should be slightly more sweet than sour or salty.
5 Add water to sauce while cooking, to maintain the consistency you require.
6 Garnish with chopped coriander leaves. Serve with Thai snacks, particularly crisp-fried food. This sauce will keep in sterilised jars for several weeks in the refrigerator.
Note: Available in jars in Asian stores, sometimes called 'salted' plums.

MAKES 2 TO 3 CUPS
(500 TO 750 ML/16 FL OZ TO 1¼ PTS)

PRAWN (SHRIMP) AND PORK DIP

KAO TANG

Kao Tang is actually the name of the crispy shavings of overcooked rice caught on the base of the saucepan or rice cooker when scraping out the pan. They are saved, prized and used as crispy rice biscuits to eat with spicy dips like the prawn and pork recipe below. Gim Ping — or the crispy prawn crackers you deep-fry, available from Asian supermarkets — make a tasty alternative.

100 g (3½ oz) lean pork, sliced
60 g (2 oz) prawnmeat or mixed prawn and crabmeat
1 tablespoon chopped coriander root
1 tablespoon chopped onion
2 teaspoons chopped garlic
1 cup (250 ml/8 fl oz) coconut milk
1 tablespoon red curry paste, bought or homemade (see recipe page 31)
1 teaspoon salt
2 teaspoons sugar

1 In a food processor, mince together pork, prawnmeat, coriander root, onion and garlic.
2 Simmer ½ cup (125 ml/4 fl oz) coconut milk in a small saucepan over medium heat. Add curry paste. Stir for a few minutes until the heat releases the full aroma of the paste.
3 Stir in pork mixture and remaining coconut milk. Add a little more coconut milk if the sauce is too thick.
4 Add salt and sugar. Taste, adding a little extra of either if necessary.
5 Serve with crispy prawn crackers (Gim Ping), or fresh crunchy vegetables, such as carrot and celery sticks.

SERVES 4

CRISPY PARCELS
KEIO GROB

3 tablespoons cooking oil

FILLING
1 clove garlic, chopped
1 onion, chopped
1 tablespoon chopped fresh
coriander root
60 g (2 oz) minced pork
60 g (2 oz) finely chopped prawns
(shrimps) cooked or raw
½ teaspoon salt
1 teaspoon pepper
1 tablespoon sugar
2 carrots, grated
2 tablespoons finely chopped
shallots (spring onions)
50 won ton wrappers, fresh
or thawed
400 ml (13 fl oz) vegetable oil
for deep frying

TO SERVE
Sweet Chilli Dipping Sauce
(see recipe page 16)
Sweet and Sour Cucumber Relish
(see recipe page 14)

1 TO PREPARE FILLING: Heat a little oil in a wok over medium heat. Stir-fry garlic until golden. Add onion and coriander root. Stir-fry several minutes, then add pork, prawns (shrimps), salt, pepper and sugar. Stir-fry until pork is cooked. Add carrots and shallots. Stir several times, remove from heat and transfer to a bowl to cool.

2 Use double sheets of won ton wrappers at a time, if they appear to be too flimsy. Place them in front of you on top of a damp tea towel, as they dry out easily. Arrange a won ton wrapper with a corner towards you. Place one teaspoonful of filling in the centre. Moisten the edges of the won ton wrapper with water. Fold the bottom corner away from you and over to the opposite corner, forming a triangular parcel. Use the towel to help you (see photo). Press the edges together to seal. Twist each wing of the triangle towards the middle. Repeat until all the filling is used.

1 *Place wonton wrapper on damp tea towel with corner of wrapper towards you. Place one teaspoon of filling in centre.*

2 *Use towel to fold over to opposite corner forming a triangular parcel.*

3 *Twist wings and deep fry.*

3 Deep-fry several at a time, turning if necessary until golden, about 2 minutes each. Serve with Sweet Chilli Dipping Sauce and Sweet and Sour Cucumber Relish.

SERVES 6

❖ **CORIANDER**

Coriander is an important ingredient in many Thai recipes. Try growing your own so that you always have a fresh supply.

Coriander is an annual and grows 25 cm to 60 cm (10 in to 24 in) high. It likes full sun. Seeds can be sown at almost any time of the year in moderate climates.

THAI SPRING ROLLS
POH PIA

FILLING
500 g (1 lb) lean pork, chopped into 2 cm (¾ in) cubes
100 g (3½ oz) cooked prawns (shrimps), peeled and chopped
½ small onion, sliced
1 clove garlic, finely chopped
1 tablespoon chopped coriander root
3 tablespoons vegetable oil
1 teaspoon pepper
1 teaspoon salt
1½ tablespoons sugar
2 large carrots, grated
1 tablespoon finely chopped shallots (spring onions)
20 spring roll wrappers
1½ teaspoons cornflour mixed with 2 tablespoons water
400 ml (13 fl oz) vegetable oil

TO SERVE
sliced cucumber
fresh coriander sprigs
Sweet Chilli Dipping Sauce (see recipe page 16)
Sweet and Sour Cucumber Relish (see recipe page 14)

1 TO PREPARE FILLING: In a saucepan, simmer pork with just enough water to cover for about 20 minutes, until pork is tender. This reduces the pork's fat and moisture content.

2 Drain, and blend in a food processor to a fine texture.

3 In a wok, stir-fry minced pork, prawns (shrimps), onion, garlic and coriander root in oil, until onion is golden and prawns (shrimps) are pink. Add pepper, salt and sugar, stirring until sugar dissolves. Taste to see if extra pepper or sugar is needed. Add carrot and stir briefly. Remove from heat. Place in a bowl, sprinkle with chopped shallots, then leave to cool. Now for the packaging!

4 Use a clean damp cloth or towel to keep the spring roll wrappers damp, as they dry out very quickly. Lay one wrapper on the towel with a corner towards you. Wet all the edges with cornflour and water paste. Place 1 tablespoon of filling in the nearest corner to you. Using the towel to help you, roll corner flap away from you over the mixture. Fold in side corners and roll up, using the towel to keep the wrapper smoothly rolled and damp. Seal the edges with more paste. Repeat with remaining wrappers and filling.

5 Deep-fry spring rolls in vegetable oil, several at a time, turning them over to brown evenly. Don't overcook as they become soggy inside. Drain on absorbent kitchen paper.

6 Serve with sliced cucumber and coriander sprigs. Accompany with Sweet Chilli Dipping Sauce and Sweet and Sour Cucumber Relish.

MAKES 20 TO 30

CRISP FRIED CALAMARI (SQUID)
PLA MEUK TOD

BATTER
1 egg, lightly beaten
1 teaspoon sugar
½ teaspoon salt
½ teaspoon pepper
300 g (10 oz) calamari (squid) rings, rinsed, drained and dried
100 g (3½ oz) breadcrumbs
vegetable oil, for deep-frying

TO SERVE
Sweet Chilli Dipping Sauce (see recipe page 16)

1 TO PREPARE BATTER: Mix egg, sugar, salt and pepper in a bowl. Marinate calamari (squid) for about 10 minutes.

2 Remove calamari (squid) and drain in a colander for 20 minutes. (Reserve the egg mixture for later use as an omelette if you like.)

3 Lightly coat calamari (squid) with breadcrumbs. Deep-fry in vegetable oil in a wok or saucepan, cooking several at a time, until golden. Serve with Sweet Chilli Dipping Sauce.

SERVES 4

Thai Spring Rolls with Sweet Chilli Dipping Sauce and Sweet and Sour Cucumber Relish.

RICE, NOODLES AND THAI SAUCES

Rice is the mainstay of the Thai diet. Spicy sauces are often served as a condiment and make a delicious dish out of a bowl of rice or noodles.

Unsalted, long-grain plain or jasmine rice is served with main meals. Sticky or glutinous rice is reserved for sweet dishes.

Rice is probably at the core of Thailand's apparent good fortune throughout history. The huge rice crop has allowed them to weather famines in the bad years and prosper in the good.

The Thais show their appreciation of the role the rice crop plays by setting aside a day in May to celebrate the Rice Planting Festival or Ploughing Ceremony.

Noodles came to Thailand with the Chinese. Thais like to stir-fry noodles with a variety of meats and vegetables, or make them the basis of a hearty soup!

Sweet and Sour Crisp-fried Thai Noodles (page 24),
Stir-fried Glass Noodles with Vegetables (page 27)

SPICY SAUCES

CHILLI FISH SAUCE
NAM PLA PRIK

3 large fresh chillies, finely sliced
**1 clove garlic, finely sliced
or minced**
4 tablespoons lemon juice
100 ml (3½ fl oz) fish sauce

In a bowl, stir together chillies, garlic, lemon juice and fish sauce. Serve in shallow bowls as an accompaniment to traditional Thai meals.

**MAKES ABOUT ¾ CUP
(180 ML/6 FL OZ)**

SOUR FISH SAUCE
NAM PLA MANAO

4 tablespoons lemon juice
100 ml (3½ fl oz) fish sauce

In a bowl, stir together lemon juice and fish sauce. Pour into shallow serving bowls. Serve as an accompaniment to traditional Thai meals, especially as a condiment for noodles and soups.

**MAKES ABOUT ¾ CUP
(180 ML/6 FL OZ)**

CRAB DIP
POO LON

Unlike the nam priks, which are uncooked dipping sauces (sometimes with cooked ingredients), lons are boiled dipping sauces. Lons are usually served with fried fish, raw vegetables, rice or noodles.

**1½ cups (375 ml/12 fl oz)
thick coconut milk**
**200 g (6½ oz) crabmeat
(fresh or canned), flaked**
1 medium-sized onion, finely chopped
¼ teaspoon sugar
salt
pepper
2 teaspoons tamarind or lemon juice
**2 fresh chillies, finely sliced or
½ tablespoon roasted chilli paste,
bought or homemade
(see recipe see page 29)**
**1 tablespoon chopped fresh
coriander leaves, to garnish**

In a saucepan, bring coconut milk to the boil. Add crabmeat and simmer for 5 minutes, stirring occasionally. Add onion, sugar, salt, pepper, tamarind juice and sliced chillies. Simmer until sauce thickens. Taste to see if extra sugar, salt, pepper or tamarind juice is needed. Remove from heat. Garnish with coriander leaves.

SERVES 4

FLAKED FISH WITH TAMARIND SAUCE
NAM PRIK THA DANG

4 tablespoons vegetable oil
**100 g (3½ oz) dried red chillies,
stalks removed**
1 onion, chopped
2 tablespoons chopped garlic
1 tablespoon chopped coriander root
2 teaspoons shrimp paste
1 tablespoon sugar
1 tablespoon lemon juice
1 tablespoon tamarind juice
2 tablespoons fish sauce
200 g (6½ oz) white-fleshed fish, flaked

1 Heat half the oil in a wok or frypan. Stir-fry chillies over medium heat. Remove chillies and set aside. Brown onion. Add garlic and coriander root. Stir-fry for several minutes. Remove and place beside chillies. Using the rest of the oil, slowly fry shrimp paste, browning without burning.
2 In a food processor, combine all ingredients except flaked fish, with a little boiled water to moisten if necessary. Process until well mixed but not mushy.
3 Pour into a bowl and stir flaked fish into sauce. Taste to see if extra lemon juice, sugar or fish sauce is needed. The sauce should taste spicy and slightly sweet, sour and salty. It will keep for 1 to 2 days refrigerated in a sterilised jar.

**MAKES ABOUT 2 CUPS
(500 ML/16 FL OZ)**

From left: Sour Fish Sauce, Chilli Fish Sauce, Crab Dip, Flaked Fish with Tamarind Sauce, Chilli Vinegar with Garlic and Ginger, Hot and Sour Chilli Sauce, and Spicy Dried Shrimp Sauce.

CHILLI VINEGAR WITH GARLIC AND GINGER
NAM JIM ROT DED

½ cup (125 ml/4 fl oz) water
3 cups (750 ml/1¼ pts) vinegar
½ cup (125 ml/4 fl oz) fish sauce
3 tablespoons sugar
1 teaspoon salt
1 kg (2 lb) fresh red chillies
(preferably small hot ones),
stems removed
4 tablespoons, chopped garlic
4 tablespoons sliced fresh
ginger root
4 tablespoons chopped whole
coriander plant including root

1 In a large saucepan, bring water, vinegar, fish sauce, sugar and salt to the boil. Boil for 30 seconds. Remove from heat. Taste to see if sauce needs extra vinegar, sugar or salt. Stand saucepan in a tray of cold water to cool.
2 In a food processor, blend chillies, garlic, ginger and coriander until fine. Pour this paste into the cooled vinegar syrup.
3 Add more vinegar if there is not enough liquid to cover the chilli mixture or if you would like a thinner sauce. The consistency is a matter of choice, either a thick paste or a thinner sauce. Store in sterilised glass jars with tightly fitting lids.

**MAKES ABOUT 6 CUPS
(1.5 LITRES/2½ PINTS)**

HOT AND SOUR CHILLI SAUCE
NAM PRIK KEEGA

This chilli sauce is delicious with barbecued prawns (shrimps), fish and pork but is also eaten in Thailand with rice and salads.

100 g (3½ oz) fresh red chillies
100 g (3½ oz) fresh green chillies
1 tablespoon vegetable oil
1 onion, chopped
2 tablespoons chopped garlic
1 tablespoon chopped
coriander root
1 tablespoon lemon juice
1 tablespoon fish sauce
2 tablespoons chopped fresh
coriander leaves
2 tablespoons finely chopped shallots
(spring onions)

1 Remove stalks from chillies. Stir-fry chillies briefly in oil. Remove and set aside. Add onion, garlic and coriander root, stir-frying for several minutes. Remove from heat.
2 In a food processor, carefully process chillies, onion, garlic and coriander root so that the sauce is not too mushy.
3 Place mixture in a bowl. Stir in lemon juice and fish sauce. If the sauce is too thick, add a little boiled water. Taste to see if extra fish sauce or lemon juice is needed. There should be a balance between hot, sour and salty flavours.
4 Stir in coriander leaves and shallots just before serving. This sauce will last several weeks in the refrigerator, providing you don't add the coriander or shallots until just before serving.

**MAKES ABOUT 2½ CUPS
(600 ML/20 FL OZ)**

SPICY DRIED SHRIMP SAUCE
NAM PRIK KAPI

An old-fashioned style of spicy sauce to accompany deep-fried fish, omelettes, soups, vegetables or plain rice.

2 tablespoons shrimp paste
3 cloves garlic, chopped
5 fresh red chillies
2 whole coriander plants, finely
chopped (keep some leaves
separate, for garnish)
2 tablespoons dried shrimp, ground
2 tablespoons lemon juice
2 tablespoons sugar
1 tablespoon boiled water

1 Wrap shrimp paste in aluminium foil. Dry-fry on each side for several minutes. Remove and discard foil.
2 Using a mortar and pestle, pound shrimp paste with garlic, 4 chillies, coriander roots and stems, and the dried ground shrimp. Add the final chilli. Pound lightly so it is slightly bruised but not mushy.
3 Place in a serving bowl. Stir in lemon juice, sugar and boiled water. Taste to see if extra sugar or lemon juice is needed. Serve garnished with the reserved chopped coriander leaves.

**MAKES ABOUT 1¼ CUPS
(300 ML/10 FL OZ)**

SWEET AND SOUR CRISP-FRIED THAI NOODLES

MEE GROB

220 g (7 oz) rice vermicelli (dried weight not cooked)

3 cups (750 ml/1¼ pts) vegetable oil

2 eggs, beaten

1 knob pickled garlic, sliced and stir-fried until golden (see Note)

100 g (3½ oz) lean pork, finely sliced

100 g (3½ oz) green prawns (shrimps), peeled and deveined

2 tablespoons bottled tomato sauce (ketchup)

2 tablespoons sugar

2 tablespoons lemon juice

1 tablespoon sliced grapefruit peel

1 tablespoon fish sauce

4 tablespoons shallots (spring onions) or garlic chives, sliced into 2.5 cm (1 in) pieces

GARNISH
fresh coriander leaves
sliced fresh red chilli
shallot curls

1 Break up the noodles inside a plastic bag. Heat oil in a wok until very hot. Deep-fry noodles in small batches. Be vigilant, as the noodles puff up very quickly. Remove them immediately with a slotted spoon and place on absorbent kitchen paper to drain.
2 Set noodles aside. Drain off most of the oil and reserve for another time, leaving about 3 tablespoons in the wok.
3 In another pan, make a very thin omelette from the beaten egg. When cooked, fold omelette several times, place on a chopping board and cut into fine strips. Set aside.
4 Take half the pickled garlic and stir-fry it in remaining oil in the wok. Add pork and stir-fry until golden. Add prawns (shrimps) and cook briefly until they turn pink.

5 Add tomato sauce (ketchup), sugar, lemon juice, grapefruit peel and fish sauce. Stir-fry until sugar dissolves and peel turns golden. Add crisp-fried noodles. Toss several times, sprinkle with chopped shallots and turn out onto serving platter.
6 Garnish with omelette strips, coriander leaves, chilli, shallot curls and remaining garlic.
Note: Pickled garlic can be bought in most Asian food stores, or you can make your own (see recipe page 83).

SERVES 4

STEAMED CHICKEN RICE

KHAO MAN GAI

4 tablespoons vegetable oil

4 cloves garlic

1 tablespoon chopped coriander root

1 teaspoon white pepper

4 chicken breasts, sliced into strips

400 g (13 oz) uncooked rice

4 cups (1 litre/1¾ pts) Thai chicken stock (see recipe page 34)

sliced cucumber and chopped fresh coriander leaves, to garnish

1 Heat oil in a heavy-based saucepan. Stir-fry garlic until golden. Add coriander, pepper and chicken slices. Stir-fry until chicken is cooked. Remove chicken and put aside, leaving oily sauce in pan.
2 Add uncooked rice. Stir-fry for 3 to 4 minutes. Pour in chicken stock. Simmer slowly until liquid is level with the surface of the rice. Cover, turn off heat and stand for 10 minutes.
3 When ready to serve, remove lid, fluff up rice with a fork and arrange in a mound on a serving dish. Cover with chicken slices. Garnish with sliced cucumber and chopped coriander leaves. Serve with a spicy hot sauce.

SERVES 4

THAI FRIED RICE

KHAO PAD

This dish can be a meal in itself or the centrepiece to a dinner. Allow about 220 g (7 oz) cooked rice per person.

100 ml (3½ fl oz) vegetable oil

3 medium-sized onions, finely chopped

3 cloves garlic, finely chopped

1 teaspoon sugar

1 tablespoon red curry paste or 1 tablespoon bottled chilli or tabasco sauce

500 g (1 lb) cooked peeled prawns (shrimps), beef, pork, chicken or ham (any combination)

3 eggs, lightly beaten

880 g (1¾ lb) cooked rice, preferably cooked the day before and chilled

2 tablespoons fish sauce

1 capsicum (pepper), sliced

50 g (2 oz) green beans, finely sliced

1 tomato, chopped

2 tablespoons chopped shallots (spring onions)

GARNISH
cucumber slices, chilli flowers, shallot curls or fresh coriander leaves

1 Heat oil in a large wok over medium heat. Stir-fry onions and garlic until garlic is golden. Add sugar and stir to dissolve; if using curry paste, add and stir-fry. Stir in prawns (shrimps) and meat pieces. Push to one side.
2 Using a little more oil if necessary, add beaten eggs. Wait a few moments for them to set, then slightly scramble them.
3 Add rice. Stir-fry until heated through. Sprinkle with chilli sauce, if using it, and fish sauce. Add capsicum, beans, tomato and shallots (spring onions). Stir-fry briefly to heat through. Don't overcook.
4 Taste to see if extra fish sauce or a touch of sugar is needed. Remove and serve with garnishes of your choice.

SERVES 4

Thai Fried Rice — a delicious and nutritious meal on its own or a dish to feature at a Thai banquet.

1 *Stir-fry onions and garlic. Add prawns (shrimps) and meat pieces.*

2 *Push to one side, add beaten eggs and scramble.*

3 *Add cooked rice and stir-fry until heated through.*

Clockwise from left: Sticky rice, the most pearly white of these wholesome grains, is aromatic, slightly greasy to touch before it's cooked and needs lots of rinsing to remove all the starch; short-grain rice; and the most popular rice in Thailand today, long-grain rice. The Thais never salt their rice while it's cooking. They eat it unsalted.

2 Line a saucepan steamer or bamboo basket with cheese cloth or similar fine-weave cotton cloth. Put rice in the steamer. Steam for 45 minutes until rice is tender and translucent. Remove from heat. Fluff up with a fork.

SERVES 4

SIMPLE FRIED RICE
KHAO PAD TAMADA

This is a sweet fried rice which is simple to make. It's ideal as a light snack, or as a bed for roast duck or roast pork pieces. Khao Pad Tamada literally means 'ordinary fried rice' and it's very common in Thailand, almost as common as the ingredient that gives it its colour, tomato sauce (ketchup).

3 tablespoons vegetable oil
2 cloves garlic, finely chopped
1 onion, finely chopped
3 tablespoons dried shrimp, soaked 5 minutes and drained
150 g (5 oz) any meat, cooked and cut into bite-sized pieces
4 tablespoons bottled tomato sauce (ketchup)
1 teaspoon sugar
pinch salt
500 g (1 lb) cooked rice (preferably chilled overnight)
2 eggs, lightly beaten
1 tomato, diced
½ capsicum (pepper), chopped
fresh coriander leaves, to garnish

1 Heat oil in large wok over medium heat. Stir-fry garlic and onion until garlic is golden. Add dried shrimp, meat pieces, tomato sauce (ketchup), sugar and salt. Stir-fry for about 1 minute then add rice. Stir well to combine.
2 Push rice to one side of wok. Add a little more oil and pour in beaten eggs. Allow to set slightly, then scramble. Stir eggs through rice. Stir in tomato and capsicum. Remove from heat. Garnish with chopped coriander leaves.

SERVES 4

STICKY RICE
KHAO NIEO

Sticky Rice can be eaten as an accompaniment to a main meal, or as a dessert with added coconut milk and fruit.

200 g (6½ oz) glutinous (sticky) rice
water, for steaming

1 Rinse rice several times until water runs clear. Soak in water for 12 hours or overnight, then drain.

STEAMED RICE
KHAO PLOW

400 g (13 oz) long-grain plain or jasmine rice
3½ cups (850 ml/1½ pt) water (depends on saucepan size)
little vegetable oil (optional)

1 Rinse rice in a colander. Drain and place in a heavy-based saucepan with a tight-fitting lid. Add enough water to cover the rice by about 2.5 cm (1 in). The Thais call it about one knuckle length. If you like, add a few drops of vegetable oil and stir, so the rice doesn't stick to the bottom; don't add salt.
2 Bring to the boil. Simmer rapidly until the water is level with the surface of the rice. When tunnels or bubbles appear on the top of the rice, cover tightly and turn the heat down to very low, or, if you have an electric hotplate, turn it off and leave the saucepan on the warm hotplate. Don't remove the lid for at least 10 minutes, which is about the time needed for the rice to absorb all the water. Just before serving, remove the lid and fluff up the rice with a fork.

SERVES 6

STIR-FRIED GLASS NOODLES WITH VEGETABLES
PAD WOON SEN

150 g (5 oz) cellophane noodles
(dried weight not cooked)
3 tablespoons vegetable oil
1 clove garlic, finely chopped
1 carrot, thinly sliced
3 tablespoons water or stock
½ small stalk celery, sliced
50 g (2 oz) Chinese cabbage,
shredded
1 tablespoon oyster sauce
1 tablespoon fish sauce
1 teaspoon sugar
pinch pepper

1 Soak noodles in warm water for
5 minutes. Drain well. Set aside.
2 Heat oil in a wok. Stir-fry garlic
until golden. Add carrot and stir-fry for
1 minute. Add water, celery, cabbage,
sauces, sugar and pepper. Stir gently.
Cook for 1 to 2 minutes.
3 Add noodles. Toss so ingredients
combine well and noodles heat through.
Serve immediately.

SERVES 4

*Clockwise from left: Thick wet rice noodles,
available fresh at Asian food stores, are sold in
folded sheets for you to slice into strips or
squares. There are many varieties of dried
noodles, like the tangled threads of cellophane
noodles made from mung beans, rice-stick noodles
and bundles of egg noodles.*

CHIANG MAI NOODLES
KHAO SOI CHIANG MAI

1 large onion, finely sliced
⅔ cup (165 ml/5½ fl oz)
vegetable oil
6 large cloves garlic, finely sliced
4 tablespoons red curry paste
500 g (1 lb) lean chicken or pork,
finely chopped or minced
2 tablespoons sugar
3 tablespoons fish sauce
200 g (6½ oz) egg noodles or
spaghetti (dried weight not cooked)

GARNISH
4 tablespoons finely chopped
shallots (spring onions)
4 tablespoons finely chopped
fresh coriander

SIDE DISHES
3 tablespoons dried chilli flakes
soaked in 4 tablespoons warmed
vinegar
4 tablespoons fish sauce mixed
with 2 tablespoons lemon juice

1 Fry onion in 1 tablespoon vegetable
oil in a wok. Stir-fry until golden.
Remove, drain and set aside. In another
tablespoon of oil, fry garlic until crisp
and golden. Remove, drain and set
aside. Reserve as garnish.
2 In a wok or large frypan heat
remaining ½ cup (125 ml/4 fl oz)
vegetable oil. Stir-fry curry paste for
1 to 2 minutes. Add chicken, sugar and
fish sauce. Stir-fry for several minutes.
If chicken is very moist, allow the water
to evaporate, frying over a hot flame so
sauce remains oily. Turn off heat and
set aside.

3 Bring 1.5 to 2 litres (2½ to 3½ pt)
water to the boil in a large saucepan.
Cook noodles to desired tenderness,
about 10 minutes, then drain. Reheat
chicken in wok.
4 Serve noodles in individual bowls,
covering them with chicken and sauce.
Garnish with reserved fried onion and
garlic, fresh shallots and coriander.
Serve with side bowls of dried chilli
flakes soaked in warm vinegar, and fish
sauce mixed with lemon juice.

SERVES 4

❖ STEAM RICE IN YOUR MICROWAVE

1 Place the rice, with a knuckle length of tap water to cover it, in a ceramic casserole with a loosely fitting lid.

2 Cook covered, on high for about 12 minutes. Stand, still covered, for another 6 minutes. Times vary with this method, depending on microwave size and wattage. Check after 10 minutes on high, to see if the liquid has been absorbed.

THAI FRIED NOODLES
PAD THAI

This is a universal favourite among lovers of Thai food and in Thailand is a popular midday snack. It has become a signature dish at Thai restaurants around the world and varies enormously. If you don't have pork on hand, substitute chicken; even without the meat, the dish loses little of its appeal.

4 tablespoons vegetable oil
2 cloves garlic, finely chopped
100 g (3½ oz) sliced raw pork
4 large green prawns (shrimps), peeled, deveined, with tails intact
1 tablespoon dried shrimp
2 tablespoons pickled white radish, finely chopped (optional)
50 g (2 oz) beancurd, diced
3 tablespoons lemon juice
3 tablespoons fish sauce
3 tablespoons sugar
150 g (5 oz) rice-stick noodles, thicker ones preferably, soaked at least 15 minutes in warm water, then drained well
2 eggs, beaten
50 g (2 oz) bean sprouts
3 tablespoons crushed peanuts
2 tablespoons chopped garlic chives or shallots (spring onions)
2 tablespoons chopped fresh coriander leaves

A very popular everyday meal — Thai Fried Noodles. Experiment, to create your own signature version, as restaurants around the world have done.

GARNISH
½ teaspoon Roasted Chilli Powder or Flakes (see recipe page 29), optional lemon or lime wedges

1 Heat oil in a wok. Gently stir-fry garlic until golden. Add pork, increase heat and fry until cooked. Add prawns (shrimps), dried shrimp and pickled radish and continue to stir-fry. Stir in beancurd. Reduce heat. Add lemon juice, fish sauce and sugar, stirring to dissolve. Add noodles and stir through briefly.

2 Push to one side and, adding a little more oil if necessary, quickly add beaten eggs. Once they begin to set, gently scramble them, still keeping them to one side.

3 Place most of the bean sprouts and a handful of crushed peanuts, garlic chives and coriander leaves on top of the noodles. Stir these, with scrambled eggs, through the noodles.

4 Serve on a large plate with little mounds of chilli flakes if using, the remaining bean sprouts, peanuts, garlic chives, coriander and the lemon wedges.

SERVES 4

ROASTED CHILLI PASTE

NAM PRIK PAO

There are many variations of Roasted Chilli Paste. The traditional method requires the ashes of a fire to roast the garlic and onions until they're black. There are several good quality commercial brands available in Asian food stores and these are acceptable substitutes or you can make your own. Open the kitchen windows wide and prepare for a smoke out. The end result is worth it. This paste is an ingredient in several Thai dishes, the most famous ones being the Tom Yam soups. It can also be used as a condiment for rice, vegetables and salads, and is an interesting, if pungent, spread for toast. Use sparingly.

6 large cloves garlic, unpeeled
2 onions, unpeeled
2 teaspoons shrimp paste
6 large dried red chillies
2 tablespoons ground dried shrimp
3 tablespoons brown sugar
2 teaspoons tamarind concentrate mixed with 2 tablespoons hot water
2 tablespoons vegetable oil

1 In a heavy-based iron pan, dry-fry garlic and onions over high heat until charred. Cool, discard skins, and chop roughly.
2 Wrap shrimp paste in aluminium foil. Dry-fry in same pan for several minutes on each side. Cool and unwrap. Process garlic, onions, shrimp paste, chillies, ground dried shrimp, sugar and tamarind mixture into a smooth paste, using a food processor, blender or mortar and pestle. If necessary, add 1 tablespoon vegetable oil to help bind ingredients together.

3 Fry resulting paste in oil in a saucepan, gently stirring so paste doesn't catch or burn. Taste to see if extra tamarind juice, sugar or any salt is required to balance flavours.
4 Cook for several minutes, then cool and place in a sterilised jar with a tightly fitting lid. This paste keeps for several months refrigerated.

MAKES ABOUT 200 ML (6½ FL OZ)

FRIED RICE WITH BASIL

KHAO PAD KRAPAO

4 tablespoons vegetable oil
3 cloves garlic, finely chopped
1 tablespoon chopped fresh chilli
200 g (6½ oz) fresh chicken, pork or prawns (shrimps), cut into bite-sized pieces
500 g (1 lb) cooked rice, preferably chilled overnight
1 tablespoon sugar
1 tablespoon fish sauce
1 tablespoon soy sauce
2 tablespoons chopped shallots (spring onions)
4 tablespoons fresh basil leaves
1 tablespoon chopped fresh coriander leaves

1 Heat oil in a wok or frypan. Stir-fry garlic until golden. Add chilli and chicken, stir-frying until cooked.
2 Add cooked rice, sugar, fish and soy sauces. Cook over medium heat, stirring and tossing gently. When mixture is well combined, stir through shallots, basil leaves and coriander. Cook another minute, then serve.

SERVES 4

❖ **CHILLIES**

Chillies are part of the capsicum (pepper) family. Generally, the smaller the chilli the hotter the taste. If you prefer your food slightly milder then cut down the amount of chilli in your recipes. Gradually you will find that your tolerance for the 'hotness' increases.

ROASTED CHILLI POWDER OR FLAKES

PRIK PAO, PRIK PON

When recipes call for dried chilli powder or flakes, it's easy to make your own if you have a blender, spice grinder or food processor and some dried chillies.

100 g (3½ oz) dried red chillies (also called small or party chillies)

1 Preheat oven to 200°C (400°F).
2 Remove stems from chillies. Dry-fry or roast chillies in the oven until brown. Blend briefly if you want flakes, or process until they become a fine powder. Store in an airtight container.
3 Serve in a side bowl to sprinkle on noodle dishes, soups and salads, or mix 1 tablespoon chilli flakes with 2 tablespoons warm vinegar. Chilli flakes and vinegar make a fine condiment to go with noodle soups.

THAI CURRY PASTES

The first sound of morning throughout much of Thailand is a dull, rhythmic thump —
the pounding of wooden pestle on granite mortar. The day's curry pastes are being prepared.

A mixture of dried spices and fresh herbs, the pastes are usually combined with coconut milk, citrus leaves,
chillies and a small proportion of meat or vegetables. The creamy rich curry sauces are eaten with lots
of steamed rice, balancing the meal and alleviating the pain of searing hot chillies.

*An inexpensive Thai mortar and pestle and some
ingredients for making your authentic Thai curry
pastes — onions, limes, dried red chillies, dried
galangal, fresh hot green chillies, cinnamon sticks,
fresh lemon grass, coriander seeds, cloves, peppercorns,
ground coriander, garlic, cumin seeds, cardamom pods,
fresh coriander roots and shrimp paste.*

GREEN CURRY PASTE

KRUANG GAENG KEOW WAN

4 tablespoons roughly chopped
lemon grass
1 tablespoon fresh galangal
(or if dried, soaked for
30 minutes in hot water)
2 tablespoons chopped garlic
1 onion, chopped
2 whole coriander plants,
including roots and stems, chopped
1 teaspoon chopped lime or lemon zest
15 fresh green chillies
10 black peppercorns, cracked
2 teaspoons ground coriander
2 teaspoons ground cumin
2 teaspoons shrimp paste
1 teaspoon salt
3 cloves
3 bay leaves
2 tablespoons vegetable oil

1 Blend or process all the ingredients
together, using extra oil if necessary to
achieve a smooth paste.
2 Store half in a clean jar in the
refrigerator, where it will last for several
weeks. Freeze the remainder in measured
amounts for later use. Most curries
require about 1 to 2 tablespoons.

MAKES 1 CUP (250 ML/8 FL OZ)

RED CURRY PASTE

KRUANG GAENG PED

15 dried red chillies
10 black peppercorns
1 tablespoon ground coriander
1 tablespoon ground cumin
1 teaspoon salt
4 whole cloves
3 bay leaves
1 teaspoon ground nutmeg
1 onion, chopped
2 tablespoons chopped garlic
4 tablespoons roughly chopped
lemon grass
1 tablespoon fresh galangal
(or if dried, soaked 30 minutes
in hot water)
4 tablespoons chopped
coriander root
2 tablespoons chopped lime zest
2 teaspoons shrimp paste
2 tablespoons vegetable oil

1 Grind chillies, peppercorns, coriander,
cumin, salt, cloves, bay leaves and
nutmeg in a blender or spice mill.
Combine with onion, garlic, lemon grass,
galangal, coriander root, lime zest, shrimp
paste and vegetable oil in a food processor.
2 When you've made a smooth reddish
brown paste, refrigerate half of it in a
clean tightly lidded jar, and freeze the
rest in measured amounts, of about 1½
tablespoons each.

MAKES ABOUT 300 ML (10 FL OZ)

MUSSAMAN (MUSLIM) CURRY PASTE

KRUANG GAENG MUSSAMAN

8 large dried red chillies, stems removed
5 cloves
2 teaspoons ground cinnamon or 1 stick
6 cardamom seeds or 3 cardamom pods
½ teaspoon ground or grated nutmeg
3 bay leaves
1 tablespoon coriander, ground
or in seeds
1 tablespoon cumin, ground or in seeds
1 teaspoon shrimp paste
2 teaspoons sliced fresh galangal
(or if dried, soaked for 30 minutes
in hot water and sliced)
2 tablespoons chopped lemon grass
2 onions, chopped
4 cloves garlic, chopped

1 Dry-fry or roast chillies, cloves,
cinnamon, cardamom, nutmeg, bay
leaves, coriander and cumin, to release
their flavours. Don't burn or char them.
Place them in a blender or spice mill
and grind to a coarse powder.
2 Combine with shrimp paste, galangal,
lemon grass, onions and garlic to make a
smooth paste, either with a mortar and
pestle or in a food processor or blender,
using a little vegetable oil if necessary
to blend.
3 Place in a sterilised, tightly capped
jar. It will keep in the refrigerator for a
few weeks, or you can freeze measured
amounts.

**MAKES ABOUT 1½ CUPS
(375 ML/12 FL OZ)**

TOM YAMS
AND
OTHER THAI SOUPS

After rice, soups are the mainstay of the Thai diet.
They range from the humble rice soup, khao tom, to the queen
of the Thai soups, the tom yam, of which Tom Yam Goong —
Spicy Prawn (Shrimp) Soup — is the most regal.

Thais will often start and end the day with a khao tom, or rice soup,
known throughout south-east Asia as a quick fix remedy for practically
any minor ailment. A fever, indigestion, a cold or even a hangover
will send a Thai straight to a soup kitchen to sup on khao tom,
the universal healer.

Roadside vendors with their three-wheeled trolleys will offer bowls
of soup broth with a choice of meats and noodles. People help
themselves from the counter to garnishes of ground peanuts,
dried chilli flakes, fried garlic and fish sauce.

Spicy Prawn (Shrimp) Soup (page 35),
Stuffed Cucumber Soup (page 36)

Recipes in this book usually specify Thai Soup Stock (see recipe below). This is a very versatile basic stock, which can be adapted as required to use chicken, beef, pork or seafood.

If you are in a hurry, however, and have leftover stock from another recipe, you can substitute that instead of making up a fresh batch of Thai Soup Stock.

A useful habit is to make up more stock than you need for a recipe, and freeze the leftovers in ice cube form.

THAI SOUP STOCK
NAM GAENG CHUD

It's always a good idea to have at least one easy and nutritious soup on hand for an impromptu meal and, for that, frozen stock in the freezer is a necessity. Here's a recipe for basic soup stock which you can adapt for beef, chicken, pork or seafood. Chicken is the most versatile stock, as it can be used as a base for any soup, even seafood.

9 cups (2.25 litres/4 pts) water
**600 g (1¼ lb) chicken bones
(or pork, beef or fish bones)**
2 stalks celery, chopped
2 onions, quartered
2 coriander roots, roughly chopped
4 fresh or dried Kaffir lime leaves
**1 tablespoon chopped fresh
ginger root**
salt
pepper

1 Bring all ingredients to the boil in a large saucepan. Cook for several minutes on high, reduce heat and skim fat from the surface. Cover and simmer gently for about an hour.

2 Strain, several times if necessary, through a fine sieve to achieve as clear a stock as possible. Refrigerate, then remove any fat from the surface once again. The stock will keep in the refrigerator for several days or can be frozen for long-term storage.

**MAKES 6 TO 8 CUPS
(1.5 TO 2 LITRES/2½ TO 3½ PINTS)**

SPICY CHICKEN, COCONUT AND GALANGAL SOUP
TOM KAH GAI

4 cups (1 litre/1¾ pts) coconut milk
6 dried Kaffir lime leaves
**3 pieces fresh or dried galangal
or 2 teaspoons powdered galangal
(if using dried, soak in hot
water for 30 minutes)**
1 tablespoon lemon juice
2 tablespoons fish sauce
1 teaspoon sugar
**2 teaspoons roasted chilli paste or
1 teaspoon sliced fresh chilli**
**1 tablespoon lemon grass, sliced
into 2.5 cm (1 in) pieces**
**200 g (6½ oz) chicken breast, fillet
or thigh, cut into bite-sized pieces**
**100 g (3½ oz) champignons, fresh
or canned**
**fresh coriander, mint or basil
leaves, to garnish**

1 In a saucepan, bring coconut milk to the boil. Add lime leaves, galangal, lemon juice, fish sauce, sugar, roasted chilli paste, chilli and lemon grass. Simmer for 5 minutes.
2 Add chicken and champignons. Simmer for another 5 minutes. Taste to see if extra lemon juice, fish sauce or sugar is needed. If soup is too thick, add a little more coconut milk or water.
3 Pour into serving bowls. Garnish with fresh coriander leaves, mint or basil.

SERVES 4

VEGETABLE AND PRAWN (SHRIMP) SOUP
GAENG LIANG

1 tablespoon dried shrimp
3 onions, chopped
10 peppercorns, cracked
**6 cups (1.5 litres/2½ pt) chicken Thai
Soup Stock (see recipe this page)**
2 tablespoons fish sauce
4 carrots, sliced
60 g (2 oz) cauliflower florets
2 zucchini (courgettes), sliced
30 g (1 oz) sliced green beans
**12 large green prawns (shrimps),
peeled, deveined, with tails intact**
fresh basil leaves, to garnish

1 Pound or blend in a food processor dried shrimp, onions and peppercorns, with a little water to mix. Bring stock to the boil in a saucepan. Add fish sauce and the paste you've just made. Simmer for several minutes.
2 Add carrots, cauliflower, zucchini (courgettes) and beans. Simmer another 1 to 2 minutes. Add prawns (shrimps). Simmer until prawns (shrimps) are pink and vegetables are tender, about 3 to 4 minutes.
3 Remove from heat and pour into serving bowls. Garnish with basil leaves.

SERVES 4

Pork and Noodle Soup can be made with any type of noodle, rice or egg, wide or narrow.

PORK AND NOODLE SOUP

BA MEE NAM MUU

This is a very popular soup eaten at any time of the day in Thailand, at road-side vendors and at the open shop fronts of Thai 'soup-kitchens'. The soup can be served with any type of noodle, rice or egg, wide or narrow. For this recipe, we've chosen Chinese egg noodles. It can be served at home as a hearty curtain-raiser to a Thai banquet or as a light meal in itself.

8 cups (2 litres/3½ pts) chicken Thai Soup Stock (see recipe page 34)

250 g (8 oz) Roast Red Pork (see recipe page 40) or any cooked lean pork, thinly sliced

1 tablespoon sugar

2 tablespoons fish sauce

150 g (5 oz) Chinese dried egg noodles

4 cloves garlic, finely chopped and fried until crisp

50 g (2 oz) bean sprouts

3 lettuce leaves, shredded

GARNISH

2 tablespoons chopped fresh coriander leaves

1 tablespoon dried red chilli flakes or fresh chillies, seeded and sliced

2 shallots (spring onions), finely chopped

2 tablespoons roughly ground roasted peanuts

1 In a large saucepan, bring chicken stock to the boil. Add pork, sugar and fish sauce. Lower heat. Add noodles and simmer until just tender, about 5 minutes.

2 Add fried garlic, bean sprouts and shredded lettuce. Immediately remove from heat. Pour into a large tureen or serving bowl. Garnish with coriander leaves. Serve the rest of the garnishes in bowls and let people help themselves.

SERVES 4

SPICY PRAWN (SHRIMP) SOUP

TOM YAM GOONG

This delicious soup is the most famous of the tom yam Thai soups, and in Thailand is often served in a charcoal-heated steamboat. Tom Yam Goong is made with prawns (shrimps) and if you like it hot, then include fresh chillies. If there's any doubt, serve it with a side dish of chilli. Tom yams can also be made with pork, beef, chicken or fish, and for a really special meal, with seafood.

6 cups (1.5 litres/2½ pts) chicken Thai Soup Stock (see recipe page 34)

8 pieces fresh galangal

8 fresh or dried Kaffir lime leaves

2 tablespoons lemon grass, cut in 2 cm (¾ in) pieces

4 tablespoons lemon juice

1 tablespoon fish sauce

1 tablespoon roasted chilli paste, bought or homemade (see recipe page 29)

16 fresh green prawns (shrimps), peeled, deveined, with tails intact

20 champignons, sliced in half

2 small fresh chillies, finely sliced (optional)

chopped fresh coriander leaves, to garnish

1 Bring chicken stock to the boil. Add galangal, lime leaves and lemon grass. Boil rapidly for several minutes. Turn down heat to low. Stir in lemon juice, fish sauce and roasted chilli paste. Simmer for another minute.

2 Add prawns (shrimps) and champignons. Cook for another 3 minutes, being careful not to overcook the prawns (shrimps). Taste to see if extra lemon juice, fish sauce or roasted chilli paste is needed. Add sliced chillies, if using. Serve garnished with chopped coriander leaves.

VARIATIONS

SPICY SOUP WITH MIXED SEAFOOD (TOM YAM TALAY): As Tom Yam Goong, using a stock made from prawn (shrimp) shells instead of chicken, and adding a variety of seafood.

SPICY CHICKEN SOUP (TOM YAM GAI): As Tom Yam Goong, replacing prawns (shrimps) with 300 g (9½ oz) chicken fillets, cut into bite-sized pieces.

SPICY PORK SOUP (TOM YAM MU) AND SPICY BEEF SOUP (TOM YAM NUA): As Tom Yam Goong, replacing prawns (shrimps) with 200 g (6½ oz) sliced meat strips.

SERVES 4

saucepan. Stir in blended paste, fish sauce, sugar and pepper. Bring to the boil. Reduce heat and stir with a wooden spoon until smooth. Add pumpkin and simmer gently for about 20 minutes until pumpkin is tender. Taste to see if extra seasoning is required.

4 Just before serving, stir in basil leaves and reserved thick coconut cream. Garnish with a sprinkle of extra basil leaves.

SERVES 4

STUFFED CUCUMBER SOUP

GAENG CHUD THANG KWA SOD SAI

3 cucumbers
8 cups (2 litres/3½ pt) pork or chicken Thai Soup Stock (see recipe page 34)

FILLING
300 g (10 oz) pork, roughly chopped
½ small onion, finely chopped
2 large cloves garlic, finely chopped
1 teaspoon pepper
1 teaspoon sugar
2 tablespoons fish sauce

1 TO PREPARE FILLING: Process pork, onion, garlic, pepper, sugar and fish sauce in a food processor until you have a fine-textured filling.

2 Peel cucumbers, leaving some strips of green for colour. Cut ends off each cucumber then cut each into three equal pieces. Hollow out and stuff with filling. Secure with toothpicks, placed crossways, at both ends.

3 Heat stock in a large saucepan. Gently add cucumbers. Simmer for about 5 minutes. Taste to see whether stock needs extra pepper, sugar or fish sauce. Remove from heat and serve.

SERVES 4

Pumpkin and Coconut Cream Soup can be served in a large pumpkin shell.

PUMPKIN AND COCONUT CREAM SOUP

GAENG LIANG FAK TONG

400 g (13 oz) pumpkin, peeled and cut in 2.5 cm (1 in) cubes
1 tablespoon lemon or lime juice
100 g (3½ oz) green prawns (shrimps) or dried shrimp
2 onions
¼ teaspoon shrimp paste
2 fresh chillies, seeded, or 2 teaspoons roasted chilli paste (optional)
1 tablespoon finely chopped lemon grass
300 ml (½ pt) water plus a little more

3 cups (750 ml/1¼ pt) coconut milk (reserve thick cream from top)
1 tablespoon fish sauce
1 teaspoon sugar
½ teaspoon pepper
80 g (2½ oz) fresh basil leaves, reserving some for garnish

1 Sprinkle pumpkin with lemon juice and let it stand for about 20 minutes. Shell and devein fresh prawns (shrimps) or wash dried shrimp.

2 In a food processor, combine prawns (shrimps), onions, shrimp paste, chillies, lemon grass and a little water. Blend to a smooth paste.

3 Combine 300 ml (½ pt) water with thin coconut milk in a large

Rice Soup with Chicken is a mild soup that makes a perfect late-night supper.

RICE SOUP WITH CHICKEN

KHAO TOM GAI

The famous Asian cure-all, Khao Tom, or Rice Soup can be made with chicken, pork or seafood pieces. It's a mild soup eaten by the Thais at breakfast or any time of the day if they're feeling off colour. It's a great antidote for hangovers, and a fine late-night supper.

100 g (3½ oz) uncooked rice
1 tablespoon vegetable oil
1 tablespoon chopped garlic
1 tablespoon finely sliced fresh ginger root
200 g (6½ oz) lean chicken, cut into bite-sized pieces (see *Note*)
1 teaspoon white pepper
3 tablespoons fish sauce
½ small onion, sliced
1 tablespoon chopped fresh coriander leaves
1 tablespoon chopped shallots (spring onions)

GARNISH
crispy fried noodles
fresh herb leaves
sliced chillies or capsicum
chopped shallots (spring onions)

1 Rinse rice several times. Place in saucepan with water and bring to the boil. Simmer slowly, adding a little more water if necessary, so rice becomes like porridge and there is about 6 cups (1.5 litres/2½ pints) of stock.
2 In another large saucepan, heat oil and stir-fry garlic and ginger. Add chicken, pepper and fish sauce. Stir-fry until chicken is cooked. Add onion, rice and rice stock, stirring well. Cook for another few minutes.
3 Just before serving, stir in chopped coriander and shallots (spring onions). Add garnishes of your choice.
Note: Alternatives to chicken for Khao Tom include fresh prawns (shrimps), fish pieces, liver strips, duck, Roast Red Pork (see recipe page 40) and roast duck pieces.

SERVES 4 TO 6

BEEF NOODLE SOUP

GWAYTIO NUA

This soup is particularly good when made with Rich Beef Stock (see recipe page 40). Otherwise any beef, chicken or pork stock will do.

4 cups (1 litre/32 fl oz) Rich Beef Stock
4 cloves garlic, chopped
1 stalk celery, sliced
2 onions, sliced
6 dried mushrooms, soaked, stems removed, sliced
2 tablespoons fish sauce
1 tablespoon soy sauce
1 teaspoon ground black pepper
250 g (8 oz) lean beef or liver, cut into strips
300 g (10 oz) fresh gwaytio (rice) noodles, cut into strips or 150 g (5 oz) rice vermicelli (dried weight), soaked 15 minutes then drained
2 shallots (spring onions), chopped

GARNISH
fresh coriander leaves
chopped shallots (spring onions)
celery
bean sprouts
fresh mint leaves
chilli flakes or Chilli Vinegar with Garlic and Ginger (see recipe page 23)

1 Heat stock in a large soup pot. Add garlic, celery, onions, mushrooms, fish sauce, soy sauce and pepper. Bring to the boil. Reduce heat and simmer for about 5 minutes. Increase heat again and boil rapidly.
2 Place beef strips in a straining-spoon or strainer and hold in the boiling stock for no more than 1 minute. Remove and drain.
3 Reduce heat, remove any scum from the surface and add noodles. Simmer for 2 minutes, stirring to separate. Stir in shallots (spring onions), then remove soup from heat.
4 Serve sprinkled with coriander leaves, in a large tureen. Place other garnishes in bowls and the meat strips on a plate, allowing people to help themselves.
Note: The Thais usually have a bowl of chilli flakes in warmed vinegar on the table for Beef Noodle Soup, but the best condiment to serve is Chilli Vinegar with Garlic and Ginger.

SERVES 4

PORK, BEEF AND OTHER MEAT DISHES

Main meals of pork, beef and other meats are reserved for special occasions in Thailand, usually family celebrations or festivals. For the majority of people, meat is expensive, so the basic Thai diet remains fish and rice.

On an average day, Thais are more likely to eat small quantities of meat as a secondary ingredient in soups, noodle dishes, curries and salads, using the meat to flavour the dish, rather than as a major source of protein.

A trip to the butcher in your local Chinatown will give you some idea of what it's like to buy meat in Thailand. The meat at Chinese butchers is usually of good quality and you need only to specify the amount and degree of leanness to end up with a tender piece.

Roast Red Pork (page 40)

ROAST RED PORK
MUU DAENG

Roast red pork hangs invitingly in the shop windows of Chinese delicatessens together with roasted whole ducks and chickens. By the kilogram (pound), it's almost cheaper to buy it ready roasted, but here's a recipe for the Chinese delicacy, Muu Daeng, which is now often eaten by the Thais. They snack on Muu Daeng pieces, finely slice it and add it to a variety of stir-fried rice or vegetable dishes, or serve it as a simple meal with plain rice.

1 kg (2 lb) pork fillets or pork loin with bone and rind removed

½ teaspoon red food colouring, mixed with

3 tablespoons water

coriander sprigs or shallot curls, to garnish

MARINADE

1 tablespoon fish sauce

1 tablespoon soy sauce

2 tablespoons Hoisin sauce

1 tablespoon cooking sherry

1 tablespoon sugar

1 tablespoon grated fresh ginger root

3 cloves garlic, chopped

½ teaspoon Chinese Five Spice Powder

1 tablespoon sesame oil

½ teaspoon ground fennel or fennel seeds or 3 star anise, crushed

1 Trim the pork of fat. Wearing rubber gloves, rub it with the red food colouring mixture, or put pork in a plastic bag with the food colouring and cover it that way, otherwise you'll end up with red hands. Put pork aside.

2 TO PREPARE MARINADE: In a blender or food processor, combine marinade ingredients to a smooth paste. Cover pork with it, again wearing rubber gloves, and let meat stand for at least 2 hours, preferably overnight.

3 Preheat oven to 230°C (450°F). Place pork on a rack in a baking dish, reserving marinade for basting. Cook pork for 10 minutes, baste with marinade, then lower heat to 180°C (350°F). Roast for about 1 hour, basting occasionally. Remove from oven and let stand for at least 15 minutes before slicing.

4 Serve pork either warm, sliced thinly, arranged on a flat dish and garnished with coriander, or let it cool whole, for later use. It can then be cut into slices, strips or cubes and added to stir-fry dishes or soups.

SERVES 4

RICH BEEF STOCK
NAM TOM HAANG WOOA

This soup stock can be made with any meaty beef bones but is particularly tasty when made with oxtail. It provides you with more than 4 cups (1 litre/1¾ pints) of stock (or more if you decide to use extra oxtail and water), and also forms the basis for a traditional Thai casserole. For those who like oxtail — that rather humble part of the cow now finding its way into some of the best restaurant menus — try Thai Oxtail Casserole (Tom Haang Wooa).

500 g (1 lb) oxtail or meaty beef bones

1 large onion, sliced

2 large stalks celery with leaves, roughly chopped

6 small whole coriander plants with roots, roughly chopped

2 large stalks lemon grass, chopped

6 large cloves garlic, finely chopped

1 cinnamon stick

2 star anise

125 g (4 oz) sugar

100 ml (3½ fl oz) thin soy sauce

1 tablespoon black peppercorns

water

1 Place all ingredients in a large soup pot with enough water to cover the oxtail by about 12 cm (5 in).

Simmer slowly for at least 3 hours. Check water level occasionally and continue to top up, so you finish with about 6 cups (1.5 litres/2½ pts) of stock.

2 Taste to see if extra seasoning is required. There should be a balance of spicy and sweet flavours.

3 When oxtail meat is soft, remove and set aside. Allow stock to cool then refrigerate for 1 hour, or overnight. Skim fat from surface and pour stock through cotton or cheesecloth, reserving all the bits and pieces. Wrap them in the cloth to form a little bundle like a 'bouquet garni'. Discard or use it with the oxtail for Thai Oxtail Casserole (see recipe below). Freeze your rich beef stock for later use.

MAKES 6 CUPS (1.5 LITRES/2½ PINTS)

THAI OXTAIL CASSEROLE
TOM HAANG WOOA

500 g (1 lb) cooked oxtail

4 cups (1 litre/1¾ pt) stock and Thai 'bouquet garni' from Rich Beef Stock (see recipe above)

1 large onion, sliced

3 cooked potatoes, quartered

3 tomatoes, diced

50 g (2 oz) green beans or similar vegetable, sliced

3 tablespoons bean shoots (optional)

GARNISH

3 tablespoons chopped fresh coriander leaves

3 tablespoons chopped shallots (spring onions)

1 Place cooked oxtail in a large saucepan with Rich Beef Stock, and a little extra water if necessary to almost cover oxtail. Bring to the boil and drop in Thai 'bouquet garni'. Simmer for 10 minutes or until gravy is the consistency you want.

2 Add onion, potatoes and

tomatoes. Simmer for a few minutes. Just before serving, add beans and cook until they are just tender.

3 Remove 'bouquet garni'. Stir through bean shoots if using them. Serve garnished with coriander leaves and chopped shallots, with a side dish of rice or noodles, and a sauce of your choice.

SERVES 4

PANANG BEEF BALLS
PANANG NUA

500 g (1 lb) lean beef, minced

60 g (2 oz) plain flour

3 tablespoons vegetable oil

2 tablespoons red curry paste, bought or homemade (see recipe page 31)

1½ cups (375 ml/12 fl oz) coconut milk

1½ tablespoons fish sauce

2 tablespoons ground peanuts or crunchy peanut butter

1 tablespoon sugar

2 tablespoons chopped fresh basil or mint leaves, to garnish

1 Shape beef mince into small round balls about 2.5 cm (1 in) in diameter. Roll balls in flour, dusting off excess. Heat oil in a wok and fry beef balls until brown, tilting and rocking wok so balls fry evenly. Remove and set aside on absorbent kitchen paper.

2 In remaining oil, stir-fry red curry paste for several minutes over low heat to prevent sticking. Stir in coconut milk. Add fish sauce, peanuts and sugar. Taste to see if extra fish sauce or sugar is needed.

3 Return beef balls to sauce and simmer for about 5 minutes. Garnish with chopped basil leaves. Serve with rice or a salad.

SERVES 4

Panang Beef Balls garnished with strips of fresh basil leaves.

1 Shape beef mince into small round balls and roll in flour.

3 Make sauce with curry paste, coconut milk, fish sauce, peanuts and sugar.

2 Fry beef balls until brown.

4 Add meatballs to sauce and simmer.

Stir-fried Pork and Green Beans — Thais often use snake beans for this recipe.

3 tablespoons Thai Soup Stock
(see recipe page 34) or water
3 tablespoons chopped shallots
(spring onions)
3 tablespoons finely sliced
capsicum (pepper)
1 tablespoon chopped fresh
basil leaves

1 Heat oil in a wok or frypan. Stir-fry garlic until golden. Add chilli. Cook for about 1 minute. Add beef, fish and oyster sauces and salt, stirring slowly.

2 Pour in stock and simmer meat for several minutes until tender. Stir through shallots, capsicum and basil. Stir-fry for about 30 seconds. Remove from heat. Serve with rice.

SERVES 4

STIR-FRIED PORK AND GREEN BEANS

MUU PAD TUA FAK YAW

2 tablespoons vegetable oil
2 cloves garlic, finely chopped
250 g (8 oz) lean pork, sliced thinly
then cut into bite-sized pieces
1½ tablespoons fish sauce
1 tablespoon oyster sauce
½ teaspoon pepper
1 teaspoon sugar
150 to 200 g (5 to 6½ oz) green,
preferably snake, beans,
cut in 2.5 cm (1 in) slices
3 tablespoons water or stock
(optional)

Heat oil in a wok or frypan. Stir-fry garlic briefly. Add pork and stir-fry until golden. Stir in fish and oyster sauces, pepper and sugar. Add beans and stir-fry for 1 minute Add a little water or stock if necessary to make a good amount of gravy. Taste to see if extra seasoning is required. When pork is cooked, remove from heat. Serve with rice.

SERVES 4

❖ **FISH SAUCE**

Fish sauce is an important ingredient in Thai style cookery. It has a very strong aroma, but don't be discouraged — it will add greatly to the taste of your recipe. Fish sauce is rich in protein and B vitamins and is available in Asian foodstores and supermarkets. It lasts indefinitely and doesn't require refrigeration.

4 to 5 tablespoons fresh mint
leaves, sliced if large

1 Heat oil in a wok or frypan. Stir-fry lamb for several minutes until almost cooked. Add garlic, oyster and fish sauces, sugar and chilli. Stir-fry for another 1 to 2 minutes. Taste to see if extra seasoning is required — chilli, sugar or sauces.

2 When meat is cooked and tender, stir mint leaves through, then remove from heat. Serve with rice.

SERVES 4

LAMB WITH CHILLI AND MINT

NUA GAE PAD PRIK BAI SALANAI

3 tablespoons vegetable oil
200 g (6½ oz) lean lamb,
cut in fine strips
1 clove garlic, finely chopped
1 tablespoon oyster sauce
1 tablespoon fish sauce
pinch sugar
1 tablespoon finely sliced fresh chilli

CHILLI BEEF

NUA PAD PRIK

2 teaspoons vegetable oil
1 small clove garlic, finely chopped
1 teaspoon chopped fresh chilli
200 g (6½ oz) lean beef, sliced into
fine strips
1 teaspoon fish sauce
½ teaspoon oyster sauce
pinch salt

PORK SPARE RIBS

PREOW WAN GRADUK MUU

600 g (1¼ lb) pork spare ribs
salt
fresh coriander leaves, to garnish

SAUCE

2 tablespoons vegetable oil
1 teaspoon chopped garlic
1 small onion, chopped
2 tablespoons sugar
2 teaspoons lemon juice
1 tablespoon fish sauce
1 tablespoon oyster sauce
½ cup (125 ml/4 fl oz) bottled
tomato sauce (ketchup)
2 tablespoons diced fresh pineapple
¼ teaspoon chopped fresh chilli
(optional)

1 Place spare ribs in a large saucepan. Cover with water. Simmer until tender, about 20 minutes. Drain, cool and rub lightly with salt. Allow them to stand for 3 hours — this can be done the previous day. Barbecue or grill under a fierce heat until golden, but don't let them burn or catch. Drain and set aside.

2 To PREPARE THE SAUCE: Heat oil in a wok over medium heat. Stir-fry garlic and onion until golden. Stir in sugar, lemon juice and fish sauce. Add oyster and tomato (ketchup) sauces, pineapple and chilli, if using.
Stir-fry until mixture becomes a golden-brown syrup.

3 Remove from heat. Add pork spare ribs, one by one, covering them all with warm syrup. If necessary, add a little more water so mixture covers ribs.

4 Return to heat and simmer for 1 to 2 minutes, for ribs to absorb the full flavour of the sauce without making it too cloudy by overcooking or stirring.

5 Remove from heat. Spoon into a serving dish and garnish with coriander leaves. Serve with rice.

SERVES 4

Marinated Braised Beef with Cucumber.

MARINATED BRAISED BEEF WITH CUCUMBER

NUA OB

1 tablespoon vegetable oil
1 kg (2 lb) lean beef
(large 2.5 cm (1 in) thick steaks)
¾ cup (185 ml/6 fl oz) water
1 cucumber, peeled and finely sliced
or 1 Chinese lettuce, sliced
2 cm (¾ in) piece fresh ginger root
fresh coriander leaves, to garnish

MARINADE

4 tablespoons soy sauce
2 tablespoons vegetable oil
6 coriander roots
3 tablespoons ground black pepper
1 tablespoon sugar

1 To PREPARE MARINADE: Combine ingredients in a blender and process to a smooth paste. Smear beef with paste and marinate for at least 10 minutes.

2 Smear a wok or frypan with oil. Sear marinated beef. Add water and braise briefly until medium-rare. Remove beef and, if preparing in advance, cover with foil and reserve the sauce.

3 Just before serving, slice beef finely. Arrange warm or cool beef on a bed of sliced cucumber. Simmer reserved sauce and add ginger (either the whole piece, which can be discarded before serving, or finely chopped). More soy sauce, sugar or water can be added if required.

4 Pour sauce over beef and cucumber. Serve garnished with fresh coriander leaves.

SERVES 4

1 *Line a baking dish that will fit inside a steamer with banana leaves.*

2 *Layer ingredients in baking dish, starting with vegetables, then pork and sauce.*

STEAMED PORK AND VEGETABLE CURRY

HAW MOK MUU

This recipe, which is equally delicious made with seafood or chicken, is traditionally steamed in a dish made from (or lined with) fresh banana leaves. If you can't find any, line a baking dish with aluminium foil instead.

200 g (6½ oz) lean pork, minced or chopped very finely

1 cup (250 ml/8 fl oz) coconut milk

2 tablespoons red curry paste, bought or homemade (see recipe page 31)

1 dried Kaffir lime leaf, soaked for 10 minutes and finely sliced

2 tablespoons fish sauce

300 g (10 oz) Chinese cabbage, spinach or leeks (any combination)

4 tablespoons thick coconut 'cream', skimmed from top of canned coconut milk before it's shaken

2 tablespoons fresh coriander sprigs, to garnish

1 In a large mixing bowl, combine pork, coconut milk, curry paste, lime leaf and fish sauce and mix well. Taste to see if a pinch of sugar or extra fish sauce is needed, as once you begin steaming you can't stir in more flavours. The sauce should be sweet, spicy and a little salty.

2 Line a baking dish that will fit inside a steamer with aluminium foil or banana leaves. Place washed and drained vegetables in the bottom of the dish. Cover well with pork and sauce. Garnish with coriander sprigs.

3 Place in steamer and steam for 20 minutes. Serve with coconut cream spooned over the top, and more coriander leaves, if desired.

SERVES 4

Steamed Pork and Vegetable Curry is traditionally steamed in banana leaves but aluminium foil does the job just as well.

SWEET PORK
MUU WAN

Traditionally, sweet pork was the Thai equivalent of ham, and was made to last a few days without refrigeration. Reboiled, it could be used for several meals, stir-fried or eaten cold. We don't suggest you do that, but it can be cooked, then refrigerated and served cold as an appetiser with spicy sauce dip, or served hot with rice. Any pork can be used, but preferably choose meat that's moist — for instance, a whole loin of pork, or spare ribs cut into 5 cm (2 in) pieces.

125 g (4 oz) sugar
2 cups (500 ml/16 fl oz) water
750 g (1½ lb) loin of pork or spare ribs, trimmed of excess fat
2 to 3 large onions, chopped
1 tablespoon salt

1 In a large saucepan over medium heat, caramelise sugar and water until golden brown, being careful not to burn it. Add pork, either whole or in pieces. Coat it with syrup and brown for several minutes on all sides.
2 Add onions and brown. Lower heat, cover pork with extra water, if necessary, and stir in salt. Simmer for about 1 hour for a large piece, less for ribs or smaller pieces.
3 Watch the liquid doesn't boil dry. The water should reduce to a golden syrup which can be spooned over the whole loin or the ribs when served hot on a bed of steamed rice.

SERVES 4

SPICY THAI HAMBURGERS
LUK NUA

300 g (10 oz) beef, minced
300 g (10 oz) lean pork, minced
50 g (2 oz) green beans, cut in thin 2 cm (¾ in) slices
2 onions, finely chopped
2 cloves garlic, finely chopped
3 tablespoons finely chopped fresh coriander leaves, stems and roots
1 fresh red chilli, finely sliced
1 teaspoon sugar
1 teaspoon pepper
½ teaspoon salt
1 tablespoon red curry paste, bought or homemade (see recipe page 31), optional
1 egg, lightly beaten
½ cup (125 ml/4 fl oz) vegetable oil
fresh coriander leaves, to garnish (optional)

1 In a large bowl, combine all ingredients except oil. With wet hands, knead mixture thoroughly until it clings together well. Roll into balls and shape into 5 cm (2 in) diameter patties, each about 1 cm (½ in) thick.
2 Heat oil in wok or frypan. Shallow-fry several patties at a time for 5 minutes or so each side, until evenly browned. Alternatively, grill or barbecue them. Garnish with coriander leaves, if desired.

SERVES 4

❖ **MAKE YOUR OWN COCONUT MILK**
For the best tasting coconut milk prepare your own by soaking 150 g (5 oz) desiccated coconut in 1½ cups (375 ml/12 fl oz) hot water for 5 minutes. Blend in a blender, strain through muslin or cotton cloth and squeeze out rich milk.

RED PORK CURRY
GAENG PED MUU

3 tablespoons vegetable oil
3 tablespoons red curry paste, bought or homemade (see recipe page 31)
2 cups (500 ml/16 fl oz) coconut milk
1 teaspoon sliced fresh Kaffir lime leaves (or if dried, soaked for 10 minutes and sliced)
500 g (1 lb) lean pork, sliced
1 teaspoon sugar
2 tablespoons fish sauce
50 g (2 oz) bamboo shoots or 100 g (3½ oz) zucchini (courgettes), eggplant (aubergine) or beans
1 tablespoon chopped fresh basil leaves

1 In a wok or saucepan, stir-fry curry paste in vegetable oil over medium heat for several minutes. Add ½ cup (125 ml/4 fl oz) coconut milk and lime leaves. Simmer for several minutes, stirring frequently.
2 Add pork and cook for about 5 minutes, until moisture evaporates out of pork and sauce starts to thicken again. Pour in remaining coconut milk, sugar and fish sauce. Simmer until pork is cooked.
3 Taste to see if extra sugar, fish sauce or chilli is needed. The sauce should taste hot, spicy and sweet. Add vegetables a few minutes before serving. Cook for another minute and remove from heat. Stir in basil leaves. Serve with rice.

SERVES 4

Pork Salad with Mint, Peanuts and Ginger. Here we've chopped the pork but the Thais usually mince the meat very finely for this recipe.

PORK SALAD WITH MINT, PEANUTS AND GINGER

NAM SOD

500 g (1 lb) fresh lean pork, minced or finely chopped

2 tablespoons water

2 tablespoons lemon juice

2 tablespoons fish sauce

½ teaspoon dried chilli

1 teaspoon finely sliced fresh chilli

½ large onion or 1 small onion, finely sliced

2 tablespoons sliced shallots (spring onions), cut into 2 cm (¾ in) pieces

2 tablespoons roasted peanuts

2 tablespoons finely sliced fresh ginger root

1 tablespoon fresh mint leaves

2 tablespoons chopped fresh coriander leaves and stems

6 large lettuce leaves

GARNISH
roasted peanuts

1 tablespoon finely sliced ginger

dried and fresh chilli

fresh mint and coriander sprigs

shallot curls

chilli flowers

1 In a large saucepan, slowly cook minced pork with water over medium heat until pork is cooked through but still tender. Remove from heat.

2 Add lemon juice, fish sauce, dried and fresh chilli. Stir and when cooled add onion, shallots (spring onions, peanuts, ginger, mint and coriander leaves. Toss lightly.

3 Serve on a bed of lettuce leaves. Garnish with mounds of peanuts, ginger and chilli. Decorate with sprigs of mint and coriander, shallot curls and chilli flowers.

SERVES 4

MUSLIM BEEF CURRY

GAENG MUSSAMAN NUA

3 tablespoons Mussaman curry paste, bought or homemade (see recipe page 31)

3 cups (750 ml/1¼ pts) coconut milk

100 g (3½ oz) fresh pineapple, cut in 2 cm (¾ in) cubes (optional)

1 kg (2 lb) lean beef, cut in 2 cm (¾ in) cubes

100 g (3½ oz) potatoes, cut in 2 cm (¾ in) cubes

2 tablespoons sugar

1 teaspoon salt

50 to 100 g (2 to 3½ oz) roasted peanuts

1 teaspoon tamarind juice

150 g (5 oz) whole pickling onions or large onions quartered with their tops and bases intact so they don't break up

1 In a large saucepan, gently simmer the curry paste and 1 cup (250 ml/8 fl oz) coconut milk over low heat. Simmer for a few minutes then add pineapple pieces and stir for a few minutes more.

2 Stir in beef until it is well covered with the sauce, turning frequently. Add another cup (250 ml/8 fl oz) of coconut milk and simmer gently for 15 minutes until meat is chewy, but not tender. Add potatoes and simmer a further 15 minutes until onions are tender. Add pineapple pieces and stir for another few minutes. Stir in beef until it's well covered with sauce, turning frequently.

3 Pour in remaining coconut milk, with sugar, salt, peanuts, tamarind juice and onions. Simmer for another 5 minutes until onions are tender.

4 Taste to see if extra tamarind juice, sugar or perhaps some fresh chilli is needed to balance flavours. Serve with rice.

SERVES 4

ROAST OR BARBECUED PORK WITH SPICY DIPPING SAUCE

JITTRA MUU YAHNG

400 g (13 oz) lean pork, fillets or steaks

MARINADE

2 tablespoons vegetable oil

1 teaspoon sugar

1 teaspoon fish sauce

SAUCE

1 tablespoon vegetable oil

2 large fresh tomatoes, halved, grilled and neatly diced

1 tablespoon finely chopped lemon grass

1 tablespoon chopped coriander root

1 tablespoon fresh galangal pieces (or if dried, soaked for 5 minutes in hot water) sliced

1 tablespoon chopped onion

1 tablespoon chopped garlic

½ cup (125 ml/4 fl oz) chicken Thai Soup Stock (see recipe page 34)

3 tablespoons fish sauce

3 tablespoons sugar

1 teaspoon chilli powder

2 tablespoons tamarind sauce

1 tablespoon chopped fresh coriander leaves

GARNISH

1 large green cucumber, sliced fresh coriander sprigs

1 TO PREPARE MARINADE: Combine all ingredients, rub over pork and marinate for at least 2 hours. Roast, barbecue or grill pork for 10 minutes on each side or until cooked through. Set aside.

2 TO PREPARE SAUCE: In a saucepan, fry in oil half the diced tomatoes and all the lemon grass, coriander root, galangal, onion and garlic for about 5 minutes. Blend in a food processor with chicken stock until smooth.

3 Return sauce to saucepan and stir over medium heat. Add fish sauce, sugar, chilli powder and tamarind juice. Cook for another few minutes. Taste to see if extra sugar, fish sauce or tamarind juice is required.

4 Remove from heat and pour into serving bowl. Stir in remaining diced tomato and chopped coriander leaves.

5 Before serving, slice pork thinly and arrange in several rows on a large platter surrounded by sliced cucumber. Garnish with coriander sprigs. Serve with sauce and steamed rice.

SERVES 4

BEEF WITH BASIL, CHILLI AND GREEN BEANS

NUA PAD KRAPAO

Krapao is one of several varieties of basil grown in Thailand. It's becoming easier to find outside Thailand but any locally grown basil will substitute well if necessary.

2 tablespoons vegetable oil

1 clove garlic, finely chopped

1 teaspoon fresh chopped chilli

200 g (6½ oz) beef, minced or finely chopped

1 teaspoon sugar

1 tablespoon fish sauce

80 g (2½ oz) green beans, sliced on an angle into 2.5 cm (1 in) pieces

1 tablespoon finely sliced onion

5 tablespoons fresh krapao basil leaves (reserve a few to garnish)

1 Heat oil in a wok or frypan. Stir-fry garlic over medium heat until golden. Add chilli and cook for 20 seconds. Add beef and stir-fry for several minutes. Stir in sugar and fish sauce.

2 Stir-fry until meat is cooked and tender. Add a little water or stock if gravy looks like boiling dry or becoming too oily.

3 Add beans and onion. Taste to see if extra sugar or fish sauce is needed. Remove from heat and stir basil leaves through mixture. Garnish with basil. Serve with rice.

SERVES 4

Thai cuisine blurs the line between main meat dishes and salads. Many Thai salads and vegetable side dishes use meat or fish. Contrasting colours and textures are as important as nutritional balance.

SALTY SUN-DRIED BEEF
NUA KEM

This is a traditional favourite in Thailand, but one that's unusual by Western standards. It's usually served as an accompaniment to curries, as the saltiness counteracts their hot spiciness. It's common in Thailand to see beef fillets hanging from the balcony or on a fencepost within sight of the kitchen. The meat which has been well salted overnight is drying in the sun, and the only danger of it 'going off' results from birds occasionally flying off with it.

**1 kg (2 lb) lean beef
(large 2.5 cm (1 in) thick steaks)
100 g (3½ oz) coarse salt
vegetable oil**

1 Rub steaks well with salt. Stack in layers in a covered bowl. Refrigerate overnight.
2 Fry steak in hot oil so meat becomes crispy golden on the outside. Cool and slice across the grain, into fine slices about 2.5 cm (1 in) wide. Serve warm or at room temperature, with a curry dish.
Note: If you want to, you can dry the meat further in the sun for several hours either side. If there is no sun that day, or you'd rather not be too traditional, you can simply drain the meat after it has been well salted, and cook. The 'integrity' of the dish won't suffer too much.

SERVES 4

SWEET AND SOUR CURRY PORK
MUU TOM BAI CHAMUANG

Bai Chamuang are leaves of the Chamuang tree, and very much valued because they are found only in certain country regions of Thailand. Like cooks in Bangkok and in the south, we can substitute green spinach, silverbeet or Chinese broccoli leaves instead.

**3 cups (750 ml/1¼ pt) coconut milk
3 tablespoons red curry paste
(see recipe page 31)
500 g (1 lb) lean pork,
cut into 2.5 cm (1 in) cubes
3 tablespoons tamarind juice
5 tablespoons sugar
½ teaspoon salt
5 cups leaves of Chamuang,
spinach, silverbeet or Chinese
broccoli cut into 5cm (2 in) squares,
large stalks removed**

1 In a saucepan over medium heat, combine ½ cup (125 ml/4 fl oz) coconut milk with red curry paste. Stir until well blended. As mixture begins to bubble, continue to stir, being careful not to let it catch.
2 Add pork. Stir, adding a little more coconut milk, if necessary. Simmer for a few minutes until pork is well separated. Add tamarind juice, sugar and salt.
3 Add green leaves and remaining coconut milk. Stir gently, covering the leaves with sauce and again, being careful not to burn the sauce.
4 Cover with a loose lid or plate, allowing some steam to escape. Reduce flame to extremely low heat, and steam for 15 minutes. Taste to see if more sugar, salt or tamarind juice is needed to balance flavours.
5 Serve in a bowl with a side dish of steamed rice.

SERVES 4

STIR-FRIED BEEF WITH BROCCOLI
PAK PAD GUP NUA

**3 tablespoons vegetable oil
3 cloves garlic, finely chopped
200 g (6½ oz) lean beef, thinly
sliced into strips
1 tablespoon oyster sauce
1 tablespoon fish sauce
1 teaspoon sugar
500 g (1 lb) broccoli preferably
Asian, cut diagonally
into 2.5 cm
(1 in) pieces (see *Note*)
small amount of water or stock**

1 Heat oil in a wok over medium heat. Stir-fry garlic until golden. Add beef and stir-fry for several minutes. Reduce heat and stir in oyster and fish sauces and sugar. Cook until sugar dissolves.
2 Add broccoli, stir and cover for several minutes until cooked. If necessary, add a little water or stock to help steam. Serve with rice.
Note: Bok choy, spinach or green beans can be substituted.

SERVES 4

Stir-fried Beef with Broccoli.

FISH
AND
OTHER
SEAFOOD
DISHES

With a vast coastline and thousands of kilometres of wide rivers and streams, it's no wonder the Thais' chief source of protein is fish and seafood.

There's an abundance of freshwater and saltwater fish, and plenty of fresh crabs, prawns (shrimps), mussels, lobsters and calamari (squid).

Elsewhere, stiff packets of dried and salted fish can be bought in Asian food stores. To eat them, you deep-fry them in vegetable oil and serve as a side dish to counter spicy curries.

When recipes call for fresh whole fish or fillets, use firm, white-fleshed fish such as snapper, bream, cod, haddock or whiting.

Whole fish can be fried, grilled or steamed then covered from head to tail with a quickly prepared sauce, spicy with hot chilli and creamy coconut milk, or mild and piquant with lemon grass and tamarind.

Stir-fried Seafood with Fresh Herbs (page 52).
Create your own combination with the best value catches of the day.

❖ **PRAWNS (SHRIMPS)**

Prawns (also known as shrimps) are very much a part of the Thai diet. Our recipes usually specify whether to use large or small, cooked or uncooked prawns (shrimps). Those recipes which do not specify, are flexible: it is up to the cook to use whatever she or he has available or finds convenient. Prawn meat is also available frozen in supermarkets, and may sometimes be substituted in the recipes.

STIR-FRIED SEAFOOD WITH FRESH HERBS
AHAHN TALAY

This is a dish to feature at a Thai banquet. We've suggested one seafood combination but it's up to you. See what seafood is the freshest and best value on the day, and create your own combination.

100 g (3½ oz) fish fillets
6 mussels
1 small cooked crab
100 g (3½ oz) calamari (squid) pieces
100 g (3½ oz) green prawns (shrimps)
100 g (3½ oz) scallops
2 cloves garlic, chopped
2 large fresh chillies, chopped
1 tablespoon chopped coriander root
3 tablespoons vegetable oil
2 tablespoons oyster sauce
2 tablespoons fish sauce
1 capsicum (pepper), cut in strips
1 onion, sliced
2 shallots (spring onions), cut in 2 cm slices
4 tablespoons fresh basil, mint or oregano leaves
additional fresh herbs of your choice, to garnish

1 Wash and prepare seafood, cutting fillets into smaller pieces. Scrub mussels, removing beards. Take limbs off crab and crack shells so the meat is easy to remove at the table. Remove outer shell, clean out crab body, and break meat into edible pieces. Set seafood aside.

2 Make a rough paste out of garlic, chillies and coriander root, either with a mortar and pestle or processor. Set aside. Arrange all the ingredients so you're ready to start cooking.

3 Heat oil in a wok. Fry the garlic, chilli and coriander root paste over medium heat until flavours are released. Add seafood and stir-fry gently so the softer fish pieces don't break up.

4 Add oyster and fish sauces, then taste to see whether more fish sauce or water is required to balance spicy flavours. Cover with a lid and simmer for a few minutes if seafood needs more cooking. Add capsicum (pepper), onion, shallots and fresh herbs. Stir-fry for 2 minutes, then remove from heat.

5 Arrange on a large shallow serving platter or bowl. Garnish with your choice of fresh herbs. Serve with steaming rice.

SERVES 4

WHOLE FISH WITH GINGER SAUCE
PLA JIAN

700 g (1 lb 6½ oz) whole fish eg snapper or bream
1 tablespoon vegetable oil
1 clove garlic, finely chopped
2 shallots (spring onions), cut in 2 cm (¾ in) pieces
1 tablespoon finely chopped ginger root
1 teaspoon chopped pickled soy bean or 1 tablespoon fish sauce
1½ tablespoons sugar
1 tablespoon ground turmeric
1 cup (250 ml/8 fl oz) chicken stock or water
1 tablespoon tamarind juice
½ teaspoon white pepper
1 tablespoon cornflour mixed to a thin paste with cold water
1 tablespoon finely sliced capsicum (pepper), cut into fine strips
2 tablespoons sliced onion
2 tablespoons dried wood fungus, soaked in warm water for 10 minutes (optional)
6 sprigs fresh coriander, to garnish

1 Wash and trim fish. Pat dry. Grill, fry or steam whole. (If grilling, place on greased aluminium foil.) Set fish aside and keep warm.

2 Heat oil in a wok or saucepan over medium heat. Add garlic, shallots, ginger, pickled soy bean if using, and sugar. Stir, reduce heat and cook for several minutes until flavours blend well.

3 Add turmeric, stock, tamarind juice and pepper. Add fish sauce if using instead of pickled soy bean. Taste for balanced flavour. The sauce should be sweet, slightly salty, with a hint of sourness.

4 Remove from heat. Stir in several teaspoons of cornflour paste. Return to a low heat. Add a little more, if necessary, stirring, until sauce is smooth. Stir in capsicum (pepper), onion and wood fungus and stir once or twice. Remove from heat.

5 Using tongs, place fish on a platter. Pour sauce over fish from head to tail. Garnish with coriander sprigs. Serve with rice.

SERVES 4

Whole Fish with Ginger Sauce is so simple. Just grill, fry or steam the fish then cover with the easy-to-make sauce, and garnish.

1 *Wash and trim fish then pat dry before cooking.*

2 *Make sauce in a wok or saucepan, cooking for several minutes so the flavours blend well.*

3 *Pour sauce over fish in one movement from head to tail.*

1 Make filling by combining ingredients in food processor.

2 Fill each shell, making a mound to follow the shape of the shell.

3 Dollop egg yolk on top of each mound and sprinkle with chilli. Take care moving the crabs or the egg yolk will run.

4 Place in steamer and cook for 20 minutes.

STUFFED, STEAMED WHOLE CRABS

POO CHA

5 cooked blue swimmer crabs (or similar)

FILLING

200 g (6½ oz) lean pork, chopped
1 onion, chopped
1 teaspoon pepper
1 tablespoon sugar
1 tablespoon fish sauce
1 tablespoon chopped coriander root
2 eggs, separated
1 tablespoon chopped shallots (spring onions)
1 tablespoon chopped fresh coriander leaves
2 fresh chillies, finely sliced

OPTIONAL GARNISH

chilli flowers
shallot (spring onion) curls

1 Remove limbs from crabs. Clean out body shells, keeping them intact so they can be filled. Remove all meat from the limbs and body, and reserve.

2 TO PREPARE FILLING: In a food processor, combine pork, onion, pepper, sugar, fish sauce and coriander root. Remove from processor and place in a bowl with flaked crab meat and one egg white. Add shallots and chopped coriander leaves and mix by hand, using some more egg white if necessary to hold together well.

3 Fill each crab shell, making a mound to follow the shape of the shell. Carefully break the surface of an egg yolk. Taking about ½ teaspoon of yolk, place a dollop on the top of each mound of crab filling, then sprinkle with sliced chilli. Take care not to move the crabs suddenly or the yolk dollops will run.

4 If you find the garnish exercise a little difficult, brush the filling instead with beaten egg yolk and sprinkle with sliced chilli and some coriander leaves.

5 Place each crab, stuffed side up, in a large steamer and steam for 20 minutes. Serve with a Thai salad or fresh greens. If desired, garnish with chilli flowers and shallot curls. A variation on this recipe is Stuffed Steamed Whole Lobster. See recipe below.

VARIATION

STUFFED, STEAMED WHOLE LOBSTER (GOONG TALAY CHA): Use one large cooked lobster instead of crab. Make a slit in the underside of the lobster and clean out head, body and tail, reserving all edible meat. Be careful not to damage the lobster and leave limbs and head intact. Fill head, body and tail with the same filling mixture as for recipe above, using lobster meat instead of crab meat, and brush with beaten egg yolk.

Steam, then serve so filling is hidden under lobster, and it sits up lifelike on a serving plate decorated with garnishes of your choice.

SERVES 4

CRAB CURRY

POO CHOO CHEE

2 tablespoons vegetable oil
1½ tablespoons red curry paste, bought or homemade (see recipe page 31)
¾ cup (180 ml/6 fl oz) coconut milk
1 tablespoon fish sauce
1 teaspoon sugar
1 teaspoon shredded fresh Kaffir lime leaves
2 tablespoons Horapa basil leaves, chopped
500 g (1 lb) fresh cooked crabmeat

GARNISH

fresh coriander leaves
fresh basil leaves
chilli flowers

Stir-fried Mussels with Chilli, Garlic and Basil.

1 Heat oil in a saucepan over medium heat. Stir-fry curry paste for a few minutes to release flavours. Add coconut milk. Reduce heat and simmer for a few minutes.

2 Add fish sauce, sugar, lime leaves and basil. Taste to see if extra fish sauce or sugar is needed to balance flavours. Remove from heat.

3 Steam or heat crabmeat in a microwave or steamer, being careful not to overcook. Drain well.

4 Arrange on a serving plate, in a mound or shape of your choice.

5 Pour curry sauce over crabmeat. Garnish with fresh coriander, basil and chilli flowers. Serve with rice.

SERVES 4

STIR-FRIED MUSSELS WITH CHILLI, GARLIC AND BASIL

PAD HOI MANG PU

3 fresh chillies, chopped

2 cloves garlic, chopped

1 tablespoon chopped coriander root

3 tablespoons vegetable oil

2 tablespoons oyster sauce

1 tablespoon fish sauce

500 g (1 lb) mussels, scrubbed, beards removed

½ cup (125 ml/4 fl oz) chicken Thai Soup Stock (see recipe page 34) or water

4 tablespoons chopped fresh basil or coriander leaves

1 Pound chillies, garlic and coriander root in a mortar or process to a rough paste in a food processor.

2 Stir-fry paste with oil in a wok or frypan over medium heat until flavours blend well. Stir in oyster and fish sauces. Add mussels and stock.

3 Cover and simmer for 10 minutes until mussels open and are cooked. Taste to see if extra fish sauce or water is needed to balance flavours. Stir in some basil.

4 Remove from heat. Arrange mussels on a platter or shallow bowl. Pour sauce over them and serve with rice or a salad.

SERVES 4

RIVER PRAWNS (SHRIMPS) IN CALAMARI (SQUID) CURRY SAUCE

GOONG MENAM

This easy seafood recipe is one of Somi's favourites. She calls it 'Lady of Thailand'. Traditionally it is made with Thai scampi or large freshwater river prawns (shrimps), but any medium to large prawns (shrimps) will do.

500 g (1 lb) large green prawns (shrimps), scampi or small freshwater crayfish

20 g (½ oz) prawnmeat, minced

2 tablespoons vegetable oil

2 tablespoons red curry paste, bought or homemade (see recipe page 31)

¾ cup (180 ml/6 fl oz) coconut milk

1 teaspoon salt

1 teaspoon sliced fresh makrut or Kaffir lime leaves

20 g (½ oz) calamari (squid), minced

1 Without shelling the prawns (shrimps), use a sharp knife to slit the backs and devein, allowing a large enough incision in which to place filling. Prise the prawn legs apart and flatten each prawn slightly with the back of a knife and spatula, so they can be placed legs down, sitting on a plate.

2 Stuff each prawn back with minced prawnmeat, so the line of stuffing is raised slightly higher than the shell. Set prawns (shrimps) aside.

3 Heat oil in a wok or saucepan. Stir-fry curry paste for several minutes to release the flavours. Add ¼ cup (60 ml/2 fl oz) coconut milk, salt and lime leaves. Stir well.

4 Stir in calamari (squid). Add the rest of the coconut milk. Bring sauce to the boil. Taste to see if a pinch of sugar or more salt is needed. Remove from heat and cover with a lid or a plate.

5 Carefully steam or microwave prawns (shrimps) for several minutes until they are just pink. Arrange them on a platter. Reheat sauce. Pour over prawns (shrimps). Serve with steamed rice.

SERVES 4

STEAMED MUSSELS WITH LIME LEAVES AND GALANGAL

HOI MANG PU OB MORDIN

2 cups (500 ml/16 fl oz) water

2 tablespoons lemon grass, sliced into 2 cm (¾ in) pieces

2 pieces galangal

5 dried Kaffir lime leaves

500 g (1 lb) mussels, scrubbed, beards removed

1 Bring water to the boil in a large saucepan. Add lemon grass, galangal and lime leaves. Cook for 2 minutes.

2 Add mussels. Cover saucepan with a lid and cook for 15 minutes until mussels open. Stir occasionally.

3 Warm a serving tureen or deep casserole and when mussels are ready, remove galangal and lime leaves from saucepan and place in bottom of dish.

4 Arrange mussels on top of them. Pour liquid over all. Serve with Spicy Dried Shrimp Sauce (see recipe page 23). Dip and eat!

SERVES 4

PRAWNS (SHRIMPS) WITH GARLIC AND PEPPER SERVED WITH GREENS

GOONG TOD GRATEUM

This recipe can also be adapted by substituting calamari (squid), fish pieces or even meat instead of prawns (shrimps).

500 g (1 lb) green king prawns (shrimps), peeled, deveined, with tails intact

1 leek or 50 g (2 oz) chopped zucchini (courgette) or spinach

4 tablespoons vegetable oil

1 tablespoon finely chopped garlic

1 teaspoon white pepper

1 teaspoon sugar

1 tablespoon fish sauce

fresh coriander sprigs, to garnish

1 Flatten prawns (shrimps) slightly with the back of a spoon into a butterfly shape.

2 Halve leek vertically and soak in water to clean. Cut into 2.5 cm (1 in) pieces and blanch for 1 minute in boiling water. Drain well. Arrange to form a bed on a serving plate.

3 Lightly stir-fry prawns (shrimps) in oil in a wok or frypan. Turn them over. Add garlic, pepper, sugar and fish sauce. Briefly stir-fry, avoiding overcooking. Pour prawns (shrimps) and sauce over leek pieces. Garnish with coriander. Serve with rice.

SERVES 4

SCALLOPS WITH CHILLI AND BASIL

PAD PRIK HOI

250 g (8 oz) fresh scallops
4 tablespoons red curry paste,
bought or homemade
(see recipe page 31)
2 tablespoons vegetable oil
2 cloves garlic, finely chopped
2 fresh red chillies, finely sliced
2 tablespoons fish sauce
1 tablespoon sugar
1 cup fresh basil leaves

1 Combine scallops with curry paste and marinate for 15 minutes.
2 In a wok or large frypan, heat vegetable oil. Stir-fry garlic until golden. Add marinated scallops, curry paste and chillies. Stir-fry for 2 minutes. Add fish sauce and sugar. Stir and cook another minute.
3 Check taste. If needed, add extra fish sauce, sugar or chilli.
4 When scallops are cooked and tender, stir through most of the basil leaves. Remove from heat. Garnish with remaining basil leaves. Serve with rice.

SERVES 4

Scallops with Chilli and Basil. Take care not to overcook them.

CHILLI CRAB

POO PAD PRIK

1 kg (2 lb) cooked crabs
3 large fresh chillies, chopped
2 cloves garlic, chopped
1 tablespoon chopped
coriander root
3 tablespoons cooking oil
1 cup (250 ml/8 fl oz) water
2 tablespoons oyster sauce
2 tablespoons fish sauce
3 shallots (spring onions),
cut into 2 cm
(¾ in) pieces
1 onion, sliced
5 to 6 tablespoons whole fresh
coriander leaves, (reserving a few
for garnish)

1 Clean crabs. Break into pieces, cracking shells on legs and claws so they're easy to pull apart at the table. Set aside crab pieces. Arrange ingredients ready to cook.
2 Make a rough paste out of the chillies, garlic and coriander root, using either a mortar and a pestle, or a processor.
3 Heat oil in a large frypan or wok. Stir-fry paste for several minutes to release flavours. Add crab pieces and briefly stir-fry, coating well with the paste. Add water and bring mixture to the boil. Reduce heat, cover and simmer for 20 minutes.

4 Remove lid. Add oyster and fish sauces. Stir and taste. If necessary, add more fish sauce or water to balance spicy and salty flavours.
5 Stir in shallots, onion and coriander leaves. Cook for another minute. Remove from heat and transfer to a large shallow bowl. Garnish with coriander leaves. Serve with rice or salad.

SERVES 4

Salted Fish

SALTED FISH
PLA KEM

Salting and drying fish is a way of preserving it in a country with little refrigeration outside the cities. Salted foods also have their own, sometimes acquired, appeal. Thais living outside Thailand now pay dearly for that acquired taste, because the dried and salted fish available in overseas Chinatowns and Asian food stores is not cheap.

Salted Fish is fried and eaten as an accompaniment to spicy dishes. The saltiness balances the heat of chillies.

4 x 200 g (6½ oz) whole fish, cleaned, trimmed with heads intact
3 tablespoons coarse salt
vegetable oil

GARNISH
fresh coriander leaves
cucumber slices

1 Score both sides of fish. Rub well with salt. Stack fish in layers in a covered bowl. Marinate at least overnight or preferably for 24 hours.
2 Deep-fry whole fish until golden. Garnish with coriander leaves and cucumber slices. Serve with curries.

SERVES 4

PRAWNS (SHRIMPS) WITH CHILLI, LIME AND GARLIC
GOONG MANAO

500 g (1 lb) king prawns (shrimps), freshly poached in 60 ml (2 fl oz) water, then peeled, tails intact, deveined (reserve prawn stock)
1 tablespoon finely chopped garlic
1 tablespoon hot green chillies, finely chopped
3 tablespoons finely sliced shallots (spring onions)
4 tablespoons lime or lemon juice
3 tablespoons fish sauce
3 to 4 tablespoons previously reserved prawn stock
pinch sugar

GARNISH
sliced pineapple
cucumber
tomato
bitter melon
lettuce
coriander

1 Arrange freshly poached and peeled prawns (shrimps) on a plate.
2 Mix together garlic, chillies, shallots, lime juice, fish sauce, stock and sugar in a bowl. Taste to see if extra fish sauce, sugar or lime juice is needed to balance flavours. Pour sauce over the prawns (shrimps).
3 Serve with an assortment of salad garnishes of your choice.

SERVES 4

WHOLE FISH WITH FRESH CHILLI, GARLIC AND CORIANDER

PLA LAD PRIK

3 large fresh chillies, roughly chopped

1 coriander root, chopped

2 cloves garlic, roughly chopped

700 g (1 lb 6½ oz) whole fish eg snapper or bream

1 tablespoon vegetable oil

1½ tablespoons sugar

1½ tablespoons fish sauce

½ cup (125 ml/4 fl oz) chicken Thai Soup Stock (see recipe page 34) or water

1 tablespoon lemon juice

1 tablespoon cornflour mixed to a thin paste with cold water

GARNISH

1 tablespoon chopped fresh coriander leaves

2 fresh red chillies or capsicum (pepper), cut in fine strips

6 sprigs fresh coriander

1 Pound together or process chillies, coriander root and garlic to make a paste. Set aside. Wash, trim, dry and score fish. Grill on greased aluminium foil, steam or fry, according to choice. Set fish aside to keep warm.

2 Heat oil over medium heat in a saucepan. Stir-fry spice paste, sugar and fish sauce until sugar dissolves and flavours blend well. Pour in stock. Stir and simmer for a few minutes. Stir in lemon juice.

3 Taste, and if necessary, add some more sugar, fish sauce or lemon juice to balance flavours. Check liquid level before thickening sauce. If there is not enough liquid, add a little more water or stock, stir, then remove from heat.

4 Add cornflour paste a teaspoon at a time, and stir. Don't make the sauce too thick — it should be clear and slightly runny. Return to medium heat for a few stirs, then remove from stove.

5 Place fish on a large platter. Pour sauce over it from head to tail. Sprinkle with chopped coriander leaves and garnish with chillies and coriander sprigs. Serve with steamed rice.

SERVES 4

CHILLI PRAWNS (SHRIMPS)

GOONG PAD PRIK

2 tablespoons vegetable oil

1 clove garlic, chopped

1 tablespoon sliced fresh chilli

200 g (6½ oz) large, green prawns (shrimps), peeled, deveined, with tails intact

3 tablespoons water

1 tablespoon fish sauce

1 tablespoon oyster sauce

1 onion, sliced

2 shallots (spring onions), cut into 2 cm (¾ in) pieces

1 Heat oil in a wok or large frypan over medium heat. Stir-fry garlic until golden. Add chilli and prawns (shrimps). Stir-fry to absorb flavours for 2 minutes, then add water.

2 Simmer until prawns (shrimps) are pink and just cooked. Add fish and oyster sauces, onion and shallots. Stir several times and serve.

SERVES 4

SPICY MUSSELS WITH CHILLI AND LIME LEAVES

GAENG CHOO CHEE HOI MANG PU

3 cups (750 ml/1¼ pt) water

500 g (1 lb) mussels, scrubbed, beards removed

4 dried Kaffir lime leaves

2 pieces galangal

1 stem lemon grass, chopped into 2 cm (¾ in) pieces

1 cup (250 ml/8 fl oz) coconut milk

2 tablespoons red or green curry paste, bought or homemade (see recipe page 31)

1 teaspoon sugar

1 tablespoon fish sauce (optional)

GARNISH

fresh basil leaves, mint leaves, chilli or capsicum (pepper) strips

1 In a large saucepan, bring water to the boil. Add mussels, lime leaves, galangal and lemon grass. Cook until mussels just open, about 5 minutes.

2 Strain, reserving the stock and mussels, lime leaves, galangal and lemon grass.

3 In a saucepan or wok, bring coconut milk to the boil. Add curry paste and sugar. Simmer for several minutes. Add reserved lime leaves, galangal and lemon grass. Simmer for another few minutes.

4 Add mussels, stirring sauce through them to absorb flavours. Taste to see if fish sauce is required (it may be salty enough) and if extra sugar or stock is needed to balance flavours.

5 Remove from heat. Arrange mussels on a serving bowl or dish. Pour sauce over mussels. Decorate with garnishes of your choice. Serve with rice or a salad.

SERVES 4

SWEET AND SOUR PRAWNS (SHRIMPS)

PAD PREOW WAN GOONG

2 tablespoons vegetable oil
1 clove garlic, chopped
50 g (2 oz) pineapple, diced
1 tomato, diced
½ cucumber, diced
1 teaspoon lemon juice
1 tablespoon sugar
1½ tablespoons fish sauce
1 tablespoon oyster sauce
2 tablespoons bottled
tomato sauce (ketchup)
3 tablespoons chicken Thai
Soup Stock (see recipe page 34)
or water
200 g (6½ oz) large green prawns
(shrimps) peeled, deveined,
with tails intact
2 shallots (spring onions),
cut into 2 cm (¾ in) pieces
1 onion, sliced

1 Heat oil in a wok. Stir-fry garlic until golden. Add pineapple, tomato, cucumber, lemon juice, sugar, and fish, oyster and tomato sauces. Stir until mixture turns golden.
2 Pour in stock. Simmer for 1 minute. Stir, then add prawns (shrimps). Cook prawns (shrimps) until pink and tender, adding a little more water if necessary. Taste to see if more lemon juice, sugar or fish sauce is required to balance flavours.
3 Just before serving, stir in shallots and onion. Cook for 1 minute. Serve with rice.

SERVES 4

SOUR FISH HOT POT CURRY

GAENG SOM PAY SA

7 large dried red chillies,
chopped, soaked in warm water
for 10 minutes and drained
3 large cloves garlic
1 onion roughly chopped
1 teaspoon chopped coriander root
1 teaspoon shrimp paste
1 teaspoon ground turmeric
1½ cups (375 ml/12 fl oz) water
500 g (1 lb) fish fillets,
cut into 5 cm (2 in) pieces
1 cup green beans, Chinese cabbage
or zucchini (courgette),
sliced into 2.5 cm (1 in) pieces
2 teaspoons sugar
2 teaspoons tamarind juice
2 teaspoons lemon juice
2 tablespoons fish sauce

TO SERVE
steamed rice
sliced boiled egg

1 In a food processor, or blender, combine chillies, garlic, onion, coriander root, shrimp paste, turmeric and enough water (2 to 3 tablespoons) to make a smooth paste. Add the rest of the water and blend further.
2 Heat this paste in a saucepan over medium heat for a few minutes. Add fish pieces and slowly simmer. Cover the saucepan and steam for a few minutes, until fish is just cooked.
3 Add vegetables, sugar, tamarind juice, lemon juice, and fish sauce. Cover again and simmer briefly. Taste to see if extra sugar, lemon juice or fish sauce is needed. The liquid should be salty and tangy. If it's too salty, you can add extra green vegetables or a little more water.
4 Serve with steamed rice and sliced boiled egg.

SERVES 4

STIR-FRIED STUFFED CALAMARI (SQUID)

PLA MEUK SOD SAI

500 g (1 lb) calamari (squid) tubes
150 g (5 oz) sliced leeks,
choko or spinach
100 ml (3½ oz) vegetable oil
1 tablespoon finely chopped garlic
1 teaspoon white pepper
1 tablespoon fish sauce
1½ tablespoons oyster sauce
fresh coriander, mint or
basil leaves, to garnish

FILLING
300 g (10 oz) pork, minced
1 small onion, sliced
2 coriander roots, finely chopped
½ tablespoon white pepper
½ tablespoon sugar
1 teaspoon fish sauce

1 TO PREPARE FILLING: Mince all ingredients in a food processor. Fill calamari (squid) tubes three-quarters full with stuffing. Close and secure with toothpicks at both ends. Set aside ready to cook.
2 Blanch vegetables for 1 minute in boiling water. Drain thoroughly. Arrange on a serving dish as a bed for calamari (squid).
3 In a large frypan or wok, gently stir-fry stuffed calamari (squid) in 3 tablespoons vegetable oil for about 5 minutes. Turn them now and then, careful not to break them. Don't try to brown them. Remove and set aside.
4 In the same frypan, stir-fry garlic, pepper, fish and oyster sauces. Return stuffed calamari (squid) to pan. Adding extra oil as necessary, stir-fry for several minutes, occasionally turning them over. Remove from heat. Arrange calamari (squid) on the bed of greens. Cover with sauce. Garnish with fresh coriander, mint or basil leaves.

SERVES 4

STIR-FRIED CALAMARI (SQUID) WITH PEPPER AND GARLIC

PLA MEUK TOD GRATEUM

This dish includes some green vegetables as a bed for the calamari (squid) pieces. It's important to use fresh, tender calamari (squid). Buy whole tubes (not whole squid, which is a lot of work) instead of ready-cut calamari (squid) rings, (which are often the offcuts and too tough). As a rule, tubes that are thick and spongy are more tender than the thinner ones. A visit to the local fish market is worth the trouble to get really fresh, good quality seafood. Smaller fish shops may not have the range.

200 g (6½ oz) calamari (squid) tubes
150 g (5 oz) sliced leeks, zucchini (courgette) or choko, cut into 2.5 cm (1 in) pieces
2 tablespoons vegetable oil
½ tablespoon finely chopped garlic
1 teaspoon oyster sauce
½ teaspoon white pepper
½ teaspoon sugar
1 tablespoon fish sauce
chopped fresh coriander leaves, to garnish (optional)

1 Cut through calamari (squid) tubes. Score in cross hatch pattern, then cut into 2.5 cm (1 in) squares.
2 Blanch green vegetables in boiling water. Drain and place in a mound on a serving platter.
3 Heat oil in wok or large frypan over medium heat. Add calamari

Stir-fried Calamari (Squid) with Pepper and Garlic, served on a bed of blanched leeks; Sweet and Sour Prawns (Shrimps).

(squid) pieces, garlic, oyster sauce, pepper and sugar. Stir slowly until calamari (squid) is cooked and tender. This depends on the calamari (squid), but is usually 5 to 10 minutes.
4 Stir in fish sauce. Taste to see if more oyster sauce, sugar or fish sauce is needed, to balance salty and sweet flavours.
5 Arrange calamari (squid) over the bed of greens. Pour sauce over them. Garnish with chopped coriander if desired. Serve with rice.

SERVES 4

WHOLE FISH IN RED CURRY SAUCE WITH LIME LEAVES

GAENG PLA CHOO CHEE

A quick curry dish equally stunning with large green prawns (shrimps) or lobster tails. It's a fine centrepiece for a Thai feast, but with some red curry paste on hand, is simple to make.

650 g (1 lb 5 oz) whole bream or similar fish

1 cup (250 ml/8 fl oz) vegetable oil (reserve 1 tablespoon for stir-frying curry paste)

1½ teaspoons red curry paste, bought or homemade (see recipe page 31)

1 fresh red chilli, seeded, finely sliced

6 dried Kaffir lime leaves

1 cup (250 ml/8 fl oz) coconut milk

1 tablespoon fish sauce

1 teaspoon sugar

GARNISH

fresh coriander, basil or young citrus leaves

lemon wedges

capsicum (pepper) or chilli, cut in strips

sliced cucumber and tomato

1 Wash, pat dry and trim fish by cutting off sharp spikes. Score both sides with a fork.

2 Heat oil in a wok or large frypan over high heat. Cook fish until golden on one side.

3 Lower heat. Using two tongs, gently turn fish over. Turn up heat again to cook other side until golden (about 5 minutes each side). Using tongs again, lift fish gently onto a serving plate.

4 In the wok, gently stir-fry red curry paste, chilli and lime leaves in remaining tablespoon of oil. Add coconut milk, fish sauce and sugar. Simmer for about 5 minutes. Taste to see if extra coconut milk, fish sauce or sugar is required.

5 Pour sauce over fish. Garnish with fresh leaves, lemon wedges, fine strips of capsicum and sliced cucumber and tomato. Serve with rice.

SERVES 4

MINCED FISH AND EGGPLANT (AUBERGINE) CURRY

GAENG SUP NOK PLA

2 tablespoons vegetable oil

2 tablespoons red or green curry paste, bought or homemade (see recipes page 31)

1 tablespoon fresh Kaffir lime leaves (or if dried, soaked for 10 minutes in hot water) sliced

2 cups (500 ml/16 fl oz) coconut milk

500 g (1 lb) fish fillets, minced eg ocean perch, redfish

2 tablespoons fish sauce

1 eggplant (aubergine) or 2 zucchini (courgette), diced

1 tablespoon fresh whole basil leaves

1 Heat oil in a wok or large saucepan. Stir-fry curry paste and lime leaves in oil. Add ½ cup (125 ml/4 fl oz) coconut milk. Simmer until the oil rises and liquid turns green.

2 Add minced fish. Stir slowly until fish is well separated. Add remaining coconut milk. Stir in fish sauce and eggplant. Simmer for another 5 to 10 minutes, until sauce is required consistency.

3 Remove from heat. Stir in basil leaves. Serve as a spicy sauce over noodles, spaghetti or rice.

SERVES 4

SEAFOOD OMELETTE

KAI YAD SAI AHAHN TALAY

2 cloves garlic, chopped

1 small onion, chopped

2 tablespoons chopped fresh coriander root

2 tablespoons vegetable oil

150 g (5 oz) chopped fresh seafood eg green prawns (shrimps), scallops, crabmeat or calamari (squid)

½ tablespoon fish sauce

1 teaspoon sugar

1 teaspoon black pepper

3 tablespoons chopped fresh coriander leaves

4 eggs, lightly beaten with 1 tablespoon fish sauce

1 In a mortar, pound garlic, onion and coriander root to a paste. Heat half the vegetable oil in a wok or frypan. Stir-fry paste for about 1 minute. Add chopped seafood and stir-fry until cooked.

2 Season with fish sauce, sugar and pepper. Taste for flavour. Stir through half the coriander leaves. Set aside.

3 In an omelette pan or frypan, heat remaining 1 tablespoon oil over medium heat. Pour in the egg and fish sauce mixture. When omelette begins to set, put seafood mixture in the centre and fold sides of omelette over to form a square. When omelette is golden underneath, turn it over like a pancake and brown the other side.

4 Serve as a whole omelette or sliced. If smaller omelettes are required, adjust proportions and/or cook in smaller quantities. Garnish with the remaining coriander leaves.

SERVES 4

Whole Fish in Red Curry Sauce with Lime Leaves, and Seafood Omelette. Both can be made with a minimum of fuss.

CHICKEN
AND
OTHER
POULTRY
DISHES

Chicken features predominantly in Thai cuisine. Its mild flavour combines well with fresh herbs, vegetables or spicy curries.

Poultry can be boned and served as bite-sized pieces in stir-fried dishes, curries, satays and salads, or it can be served in larger pieces, keeping the bones, in casseroles and roasts.

And yet it's cheap and readily available to the Thais, who always seem to have a brood of scrawny chooks scratching about the household.

At Thai markets, scraggy chickens and ducks, freshly killed, plucked and with the odd feather or two still attached, hang naked and indignant from hooks for all to prod and bargain over. They contrast sharply with our plump, pampered poultry, but what they lack in bulk, they make up for in flavour and freshness.

Duck Casserole (page 67)

GREEN SWEET CHICKEN CURRY

GAENG KEOW WAN GAI

If you want to prepare this spicy, sweet curry in advance, add the vegetables just before serving. This recipe is quick because it uses small, bite-sized pieces of chicken meat. However, you can use a whole chicken or chicken pieces with bones. Simply simmer the chicken in coconut milk with a little water, then proceed with the recipe, adding the pre-cooked and drained chicken pieces instead of raw chicken. Liquid can be added if you prefer a thinner sauce. This recipe can also be made with beef, pork or fish, but is particularly nice with poultry.

2 tablespoons vegetable oil
1½ tablespoons green curry paste, bought or homemade (see recipe page 31)
1 fresh green chilli, finely sliced
4 Kaffir lime leaves sliced
3 cups (750 ml/1¼ pt) coconut milk
1 tablespoon fish sauce
2 teaspoons sugar
500 g (1 lb) raw chicken meat, cut into bite-sized pieces
30 g (1 oz) drained canned bamboo shoots, sliced zucchini (courgette) or eggplant (aubergine)
30 g (1 oz) fresh or frozen peas or pea eggplant (aubergine) (see Ingredients page 5)
1 tablespoon fresh basil leaves, mint or young citrus leaves

1 Heat oil in a large saucepan over medium heat. Briefly stir-fry curry paste, chilli and lime leaves. Add coconut milk, fish sauce and sugar.
2 When coconut milk begins to bubble, add chicken, and bamboo shoots if using, Turn down heat and simmer to reduce sauce. If it becomes too thick, add a little water or more coconut milk.

Green Sweet Chicken Curry. Thais often serve their curries with a little less meat and vegetables and more liquid to flavour their rice.

3 When chicken is cooked and sauce is desired consistency, add peas and optional zucchini (courgette) or eggplant (aubergine) cooking briefly to retain their firmness. Remove from heat. Stir in basil leaves, leaving a few for garnishing. Serve with rice.

SERVES 4

CRISP FRIED SALTY CHICKEN

GAI KEM

1.5 kg (3 lb) roasting chicken
5 cups (1.25 litres/2 pints) water
3 tablespoons coarse or cooking salt
½ cup (125 ml/4 fl oz) vegetable oil for shallow-frying
fresh coriander sprigs, to garnish

1 Place chicken in large saucepan with water. Bring to the boil. Simmer, loosely covered, for about 15 minutes until almost tender.
2 Drain, reserving stock for later use, and cool. Cut chicken into four pieces. Rub well with salt. Refrigerate overnight in a covered bowl.
3 Pat dry. Fry each side in hot oil until golden, turning when necessary. Chop into smaller pieces, if desired. Serve with hot spicy dishes like curries, to counter the chilli. Garnish with coriander sprigs.

SERVES 4

DUCK CASSEROLE

TOM KEM PED

3 cloves garlic
3 large coriander roots
10 peppercorns, cracked
4 tablespoons sugar
1 tablespoon and ½ cup (125 ml/4 fl oz) water
1.5 kg (3 lb) fresh young duck, whole or in pieces
1 tablespoon soy sauce
1 teaspoon salt
100 g (3½ oz) dried Chinese mushrooms, soaked in water 30 minutes, stems discarded
2.5 cm (1 in) piece fresh ginger root
4 to 6 eggs, hard-boiled and peeled
6 carrot pieces, about 5 cm (2 in) each

1 With a mortar and pestle or food processor, make a rough paste from garlic, coriander roots and peppercorns. Set aside.
2 In a large saucepan, heat sugar and 1 tablespoon water until it caramelises into a dark brown syrup. Be careful not to let it burn. Remove pan from heat and stir in ½ cup (125 ml/4 fl oz) water.
3 Place duck in the saucepan. Return to medium heat. Coat duck in liquid and brown all over, stirring occasionally. Add soy sauce, salt and spice paste, with more water to cover the duck, if necessary. Bring to the boil.
4 Add mushrooms and ginger. Reduce heat and simmer gently for about 25 minutes. Add eggs and carrots. Simmer for a further 20 minutes or until duck is tender.
5 Spoon into a serving dish. Halve the eggs, and arrange with carrots and mushrooms on top of duck. Serve accompanied by a platter of cucumber slices, tomato wedges, lettuce, fresh coriander sprigs and bowls of steamed rice.

SERVES 4

❖ GOLDEN GROUND RICE

Ground roasted rice is added to dishes to give interesting texture and flavour. Dry-fry several tablespoons of uncooked rice in a frying pan until rice turns golden, then grind it in a food processor or with a mortar and pestle until it is fine but still crunchy — a little like coarse sand.

SLICED CHICKEN WITH CHILLIES AND CASHEWS

GAI PAD MET MAMUANG

4 tablespoons vegetable oil
6 whole small dried red chillies
1 clove garlic, chopped
300 g (10 oz) lean chicken, sliced
1 tablespoon oyster sauce
1 tablespoon fish sauce
½ teaspoon sugar
1 teaspoon roasted chilli paste, bought or homemade (see recipe page 29)
3 tablespoons Thai Soup Stock (see recipe page 34) or water
50 g (2 oz) roasted, unsalted cashew nuts
2 shallots (spring onions), cut in 2.5 cm (1 in) pieces

1 Heat 1 tablespoon oil in a wok. Stir-fry whole chillies until cooked evenly but not burnt. Remove and set aside.
2 Stir-fry garlic in the remaining vegetable oil, until golden. Add chicken slices, oyster and fish sauces, sugar and roasted chilli paste. Stir-fry until chicken is golden.
3 Lower heat. Add stock and cook another few minutes, stirring occasionally. When chicken is thoroughly cooked, add cashew nuts, shallots and whole chillies. Stir several times.
4 Remove from heat and serve. You can feature whole chillies by arranging them on top of the dish.

SERVES 4

CHICKEN SALAD WITH MINT, ONION AND LEMON GRASS

LAAB GAI

200 g (6½ oz) lean chicken meat, minced
1 tablespoon fish sauce
1 tablespoon finely chopped lemon grass
3 tablespoons water or chicken Thai Soup Stock (see recipe page 34)
1½ tablespoons lemon juice
1 onion, finely sliced
1 tablespoon chopped shallots (spring onions)
1 tablespoon finely chopped coriander leaves
4 tablespoons fresh mint leaves
2 tablespoons rice, dry-fried to golden, then ground
1 teaspoon chilli powder (optional)

GARNISH
lettuce leaves
fresh mint leaves
fresh coriander leaves
chilli flowers
shallot curls

1 In a saucepan over medium heat, gently cook minced chicken, fish sauce, lemon grass and water, stirring to separate chicken mince to an even texture. If necessary, add a little more water to keep about 3 tablespoons of liquid in the pan.
2 Remove from heat after 5 minutes or so, when chicken is cooked through but still moist.
3 Add lemon juice, onion, shallots, coriander and mint leaves. Toss gently. Taste to see if extra fish sauce or lemon juice is needed. Sprinkle in golden ground rice. Toss again gently. If you want the dish to be spicy, add chilli powder or, alternatively, serve some in a side bowl.
4 Arrange on a bed of lettuce leaves. Add garnishes. Serve at room temperature or slightly chilled.

SERVES 4

SPICY CHICKEN LIVERS

THAB GAI PAD PRIKON

300 g (10 oz) chicken livers
6 dried Chinese mushrooms, soaked for 20 minutes in hot water
2 tablespoons vegetable oil
1 clove garlic, finely chopped
2 onions, sliced
2 fresh red chillies, finely sliced
2 tablespoons fish sauce
1 teaspoon sugar
2 tablespoons lemon juice
½ green capsicum (pepper), sliced
3 shallots (spring onions), cut in 3 cm (1½ in) pieces

1 Wash and dry chicken livers. Cut into bite-sized pieces. Finely slice mushrooms, removing stems. Set aside.
2 Heat oil in a wok or frypan. Stir-fry garlic until golden. Add onions and chillies. Stir-fry for 1 minute. Add chicken livers. Stir-fry until just pink.
3 Add fish sauce, sugar, lemon juice and mushrooms. Stir-fry for another minute. Check taste to see if more fish sauce, sugar or lemon juice is needed.
4 Stir in capsicum and shallots. Stir-fry another minute. Serve with rice.

SERVES 4

Chicken Salad with Mint, Onion and Lemon Grass, and Spicy Chicken Livers.

❖ **WOOD FUNGUS OR WOOD MUSHROOMS**

Wood fungus is available from Asian grocery stores. It looks like dried pieces of burnt paper but when soaked in water turns into a jelly-like brown substance. Always soak in warm water before use.

STIR-FRIED GINGER CHICKEN

PAD KING GAI

2 tablespoons vegetable oil

1 clove garlic, finely chopped

2 tablespoons sliced ginger root, cut into fine matchsticks

200 g (6½ oz) lean chicken, sliced into strips

1 tablespoon oyster sauce

1 tablespoon fish sauce

½ teaspoon sugar

pinch white pepper

2 shallots (spring onions), cut in 2.5 cm (1 in) pieces

1 onion, sliced

½ red capsicum (pepper), cut in strips

4 tablespoons dried wood fungus or mushrooms (see *Note*)

2 teaspoons finely chopped fresh coriander leaves, to garnish

1 Heat oil in wok or frypan. Fry garlic and ginger until golden. Add chicken and stir-fry until golden. You may have to wait for moisture in chicken to evaporate, then it will lightly brown.

2 Add oyster and fish sauces, sugar and pepper. Taste and add extra fish sauce or sugar if needed. Stir in shallots, onion, capsicum and wood fungus. Stir-fry for several minutes.

3 Remove from heat. Serve garnished with chopped coriander leaves.

Note: Soak wood fungus for 1 hour. Discard stems. Alternatively, use dried Chinese or fresh mushrooms. The dried ones should be soaked for 20 minutes in warm water and the stems discarded.

SERVES 4

THAI BARBECUED CHICKEN

GAI YAHNG

1 kg (2 lb) chicken pieces, slightly larger than bite-sized (see *Note*)

MARINADE

1 tablespoon chopped coriander root and stem

1 tablespoon chopped garlic

1 teaspoon pepper

1 teaspoon salt

1 teaspoon sugar

2 teaspoons ground turmeric

3 tablespoons vegetable oil

1 TO PREPARE MARINADE: Combine all ingredients in a food processor or crush with a mortar and pestle. Rub chicken pieces with marinade.

2 Refrigerate, covered for at least 10 minutes, preferably overnight.

3 Barbecue over hot coals or grill slowly until thoroughly cooked and slightly charred. Serve with a spicy Thai sauce and rice.

Note: You can barbecue large chicken pieces and chop into smaller pieces before serving, or split the larger limbs and slightly flatten them, so they cook easily.

SERVES 4

QUAIL WITH CHILLI AND BASIL

NOK PAD PRIK

4 average-sized quail

1 cup (250 ml/8 fl oz) vegetable oil

2 cloves garlic, chopped

4 fresh chillies (moderately hot), sliced

1 tablespoon oyster sauce

2 tablespoons fish sauce

1 tablespoon roasted chilli paste, bought or homemade (see recipe page 29)

2 tablespoons fresh whole basil leaves

1 Wash and clean quail. Pat dry. With a smooth-faced mallet, gently soften and flatten them. Remove internal bone and cut quail in half lengthways. Cut each half into three pieces.

2 Heat oil in a wok. Fry quail pieces until cooked, about 5 minutes. Remove and set aside.

3 Leave 3 tablespoons oil in the wok, and reserve the remainder for later use (for another dish). Stir-fry garlic until golden. Add chillies, quail, oyster and fish sauces and roasted chilli paste. If necessary, add a little water or stock to moisten. Stir-fry for a few minutes.

4 Taste and add more chilli or fish sauce, if desired. Stir basil leaves through mixture. Remove from heat. Serve with rice.

SERVES 4

Quail with Chilli and Basil, and Thai Barbecued Chicken. Serve the chicken with any of the spicy hot Thai sauces.

1 *Prepare quail by washing, cleaning and patting dry. Flatten with mallet.*

2 *Remove internal bone and cut in half lengthways.*

3 *Cut each half into three pieces.*

❖ **DRIED MUSHROOMS**

Dried mushrooms have a distinctive flavour. They must be soaked in warm water for approximately 20 minutes before use. They are quite different in texture from fresh mushrooms and give dishes an oriental feel. They can be purchased from Asian grocery stores.

DUCK STEAMED WITH CHINESE MELON AND PICKLED LIMES

PED THOON MANAO DONG

This dish falls somewhere between a soup and a casserole. You can serve it in place of a soup at dinner, or it can be a meal in itself. The Thais believe it has excellent medicinal qualities.

If you can't find Chinese green melon (Fak-keow) at your local Chinatown, substitute chokos, or any similar bitter green vegetable. You can buy Thai pickled limes, sometimes called pickled lemons, in jars at Asian stores. Don't throw out the liquid and try not to break the skin of the fruit in the casserole/soup when serving, but warn your guests they're an acquired taste.

1.5 kg (3 lb) young duck

1 large Chinese melon, gourd or 3 chokos

30 g (1 oz) Chinese dried mushrooms, soaked in water for 30 minutes, stems discarded

2 tablespoons vegetable oil

10 cups (2.5 litres/4¼ pints) water

3 pickled limes and ½ cup (125 ml/4 fl oz) pickled lime liquid

1 small onion, halved

1 teaspoon white pepper

½ cup (125 ml/4 fl oz) fish sauce

1 Cut duck into 5 cm (2 in) pieces with cleaver and set aside. Peel melon and cut in half lengthways. Cut into 5 cm (2 in) pieces and set aside. If mushrooms are uniformly large leave them, but if they come in a variety of sizes, cut the larger ones in half.

2 In a large heavy-based saucepan that has a lid, heat oil. Add duck and cook until brown. Discard excess fat and oil. Add water, pickled limes and lime liquid. Bring to the boil. Add extra water to ensure duck is covered by at least 3 cm (1½ in) liquid.

3 Cover, allowing a small amount of steam to escape. Simmer gently for about 30 minutes, adding more water if necessary to keep duck covered. Skim surface to keep broth clear.

4 When duck is tender, add onion, mushrooms, melon pieces, pepper and fish sauce. Cook for another 5 minutes. Check taste to see if extra pickled lime liquid, fish sauce or water is needed. Serve in a large casserole dish or tureen.

SERVES 4

CHICKEN AND COCONUT MILK CASSEROLE

GAENG TOM KAH GAI

3 cups (750 ml/1¼ pt) coconut milk

1 cup (250 ml/8 fl oz) water or chicken stock

2 tablespoons fish sauce

2 tablespoons chopped coriander roots

8 pieces fresh galangal (or if dried, soaked for 10 minutes in hot water)

1 teaspoon finely sliced lemon grass bulb

1 tablespoon sliced lemon grass stalk, cut in 2.5 cm (1 in) pieces

8 dried Kaffir lime leaves

½ teaspoon white pepper

1.5 kg (3 lb) chicken pieces, chopped into 5 cm (2 in) pieces with bones

3 teaspoons roasted chilli paste or 1 teaspoon fresh chopped or dried chilli

2 teaspoons sugar

2 tablespoons lemon juice

100 g (3½ oz) whole button mushrooms, fresh or canned (see *Note*)

chopped fresh coriander, to garnish

1 In a large saucepan, combine coconut milk, water, fish sauce, coriander root, galangal, lemon grass, lime leaves and pepper. Bring to the boil.

2 Reduce heat. Add chicken. Simmer for about 20 minutes, adding more water if necessary.

3 Add roasted chilli paste, sugar and lemon juice. Simmer for another minute. Taste to see if extra fish sauce, sugar, lemon juice or chilli paste is needed.

4 When chicken is tender, add mushrooms. Cook for 3 minutes. Garnish with chopped coriander leaves. Serve with steamed rice.

Note: You can also add zucchini (courgette), eggplant (aubergine), bamboo shoots or green peas if you like, at the same time as the mushrooms.

SERVES 4

WHOLE ROAST CHICKEN IN PEANUT COCONUT SAUCE

GAI OB NAM KATI

1.5 kg (3 lb) roasting chicken

SAUCE
1 onion, roughly chopped
2 cloves garlic, roughly chopped
1 tablespoon chopped lemon grass
4 red chillies, fresh or dried
**6 tablespoons roasted peanuts
or peanut paste**
1 teaspoon pepper
1 tablespoon sugar
2 tablespoons fish sauce
1 teaspoon shrimp paste
1 tablespoon vegetable oil
1 cup (250 ml/8 fl oz) coconut milk

GARNISH
**fresh red chillies, finely sliced
into rings**
fresh coriander sprigs

1 Place chicken on a rack in a baking dish and roast at 180°C (350°F) until tender (1½ to 2 hours). Prepare sauce during the last 15 minutes of cooking.
2 TO PREPARE SAUCE: With a mortar and pestle or food processor, make a paste from onion, garlic, lemon grass, chillies, peanuts, pepper, sugar, fish sauce and shrimp paste.
3 Heat oil in a large heavy-based saucepan. Fry paste briefly. Add coconut milk. Stir well and simmer for 5 minutes until sauce is thick enough to coat chicken.
4 Place roasted chicken in saucepan. Carefully coat with sauce. Simmer a few minutes more, being careful not to break up the chicken. Remove to a serving plate. Spoon over remaining sauce. Garnish with chilli rings and coriander sprigs.

SERVES 4

CHICKEN AND PEANUT CURRY

GAENG PANANG GAI

3 tablespoons vegetable oil
3 tablespoons Panang or red curry paste (Panang Curry Paste can be bought in cans or jars in Asian stores)
2 cups (500 ml/16 fl oz) coconut milk
500 g (1 lb) chicken fillets, cut into bite-sized pieces
2 tablespoons sugar
2 tablespoons fish sauce
4 Kaffir lime leaves, cut into strips
100 g (3½ oz) roasted peanuts, blended to a paste with 3 tablespoons coconut milk
pinch cumin, coriander or salt
2 tablespoons fresh whole basil leaves, to garnish

1 Heat oil in a wok or frypan over medium heat Add curry paste and stir-fry. Add ½ cup (125 ml/4 fl oz) coconut milk. Turn heat to low. Add chicken and stir slowly until curry paste is blended well and flavours combine.
2 Add another cup (250 ml/8 fl oz) coconut milk. Stir in sugar, fish sauce and lime leaves. Bring sauce to the boil. Simmer for a few minutes. Stir in peanut and coconut milk paste. Add remaining coconut milk.
3 Check taste. The curry should be sweet, spicy and a little salty. If necessary, add a little more sugar, cumin, coriander or salt. Gaeng Panang curries should be a golden red with oily patterns on the surface. The sauce should be about half as thick as satay sauce, which is why the dish is often called 'dry' chicken curry. Garnish with basil leaves. Serve with rice.

SERVES 4

STEAMED SPICY CHICKEN

HAW MOK GAI

**300 g (10 oz) lean chicken, minced
or finely chopped**
**2 tablespoons green curry paste, bought or homemade
(see recipe page 31)**
2 tablespoons fish sauce
1 cup (250 ml/8 fl oz) coconut milk
4 tablespoons shredded coconut
2 Kaffir lime leaves shredded
1 teaspoon pepper
1 egg, beaten
200 to 300 g (6½ to 10 oz) sliced Chinese cabbage, spinach or leeks (any combination)
½ cup (125 ml/4 fl oz) thick coconut cream, skimmed from top of canned coconut milk before it's shaken
fresh coriander sprigs, to garnish

1 Combine minced chicken with curry paste, fish sauce, coconut milk, shredded coconut, lime leaves, pepper and beaten egg. Taste to see if extra seasoning is required, as you can't stir in more flavours once steaming has begun.
2 Line a baking dish that will fit inside a steamer with banana leaves or aluminium foil.
3 Place a layer of green vegetables over the bottom. Cover with chicken mixture. Top with thick coconut cream. Garnish with coriander sprigs. Steam for 20 to 30 minutes.

SERVES 4

SALADS
AND
VEGETABLES

Thai meals will invariably include at least one salad or vegetable dish. An abundance of vegetables, raw or slightly cooked, makes Thai cuisine very nutritious. Vegetables also play an important role in balancing flavours in a meal, providing relief for the mouth after the searing chilli dishes and spicy curries.

Often Thai salads have small quantities of meat and fish to flavour or contrast with the vegetables — flaked fish, ground dried shrimp or minced pork. So these recipes can be thought of as side dishes and accompaniments to a main meal, or as a perfect light lunch or supper.

Don't toss all your ingredients together. Arrange them neatly on a platter with an eye to their colours and shapes. Don't crowd too many ingredients into one salad and, if you can, decorate your creations with a chilli flower or a tomato basket or two for special dinners, and do mention to dinner guests not to eat the chilli flower!

Thai salads give you a chance to display imagination and ingenuity. As long as you're mindful of complimentary flavours and agreeable contrasts you can easily create your own salads with locally available ingredients.

This chapter also includes lighter dishes like omelettes and cold meat and fish Thai salads, which you can serve as a side dish or light meal.

Green Mango Salad (page 77), Prawn (Shrimp)
Salad with Lemon Grass and Mint (page 77).
If you prefer you can achieve a moist and milder prawn (shrimp)
salad by only slightly braising the prawns (shrimps).

❖ CALAMARI (SQUID)

Calamari or squid have a long cylindrical body and tentacles. The whole calamari (squid) (except the head) can be eaten. It is usually found in fish shops already cleaned and in this state it is a creamy coloured tube of flesh. Often it is sold already cut into rings. Calamari (squid) can be stored in an airtight container for up to 3 days in the refrigerator.

CALAMARI (SQUID) SALAD WITH MINT, ONION AND LEMON GRASS

YAM PLA MEUK

200 g (6½ oz) calamari (squid) tubes
3 tablespoons water
1½ tablespoons fish sauce
1½ tablespoons lemon juice
1 tablespoon roasted chilli paste (see recipe page 29) or 1 teaspoon fresh chopped chilli (optional)
1 onion, sliced in fine rings
1 tablespoon chopped shallots (spring onions)
1 tablespoon finely chopped lemon grass
1 tablespoon chopped fresh coriander leaves
1 tablespoon fresh mint leaves
1 tablespoon rice, dry-fried until golden, then ground
6 lettuce leaves, to serve
5 sprigs fresh coriander, to garnish

1 Wash and drain calamari (squid) tubes. Score in a crosshatch pattern and cut into 4 cm (1¾ in) square pieces. Calamari (squid) pieces are usually much more tender than ready-cut rings.
2 In a saucepan over medium heat, bring water to the boil. Add calamari (squid), fish sauce, lemon juice and roasted chilli paste. Stir until cooked and tender. Depending on how young the calamari (squid) are, it will take 5 to 20 minutes.

Check constantly after several minutes, as calamari (squid) cook quickly and can become tough.
3 Taste to see if extra fish sauce, lemon juice or chilli paste is needed to balance flavours. Remove from heat. Stir in onion, shallots, lemon grass, coriander, mint leaves and ground rice. Toss gently.
4 Serve, either warm or cooled, on a bed of lettuce leaves garnished with coriander sprigs.

SERVES 4

CARROT AND GREEN BEAN SALAD WITH PAWPAW

SOM TAM

Som Tam literally means 'sour and pounded', and that's what is so unusual about this dish. The salad has a slight tartness from the lemon juice and it's bruised or lightly pounded to a soft, but never mushy, consistency. Serve Som Tam on a bed of lettuce leaves and with a plate of Spicy Minced Beef or Chicken Salad with Mint, Onion and Lemon Grass (see recipes page 79, 68).

3 cloves garlic, peeled
1 teaspoon sliced fresh or dried chilli (optional)
100 g (3½ oz) stringless green beans, cut into 2.5 cm (1 in) pieces
2 carrots, shredded
2 red tomatoes, diced
1 small green pawpaw, peeled, seeded and diced in 2 cm (¾ in) cubes
½ cup (125 ml/4 fl oz) lemon juice
3 tablespoons fish sauce
1 tablespoon sugar
5 tablespoons dried shrimp, washed, then ground
2 tablespoons crushed roasted peanuts
4 lettuce leaves, to serve

1 Using a mortar and pestle, pound garlic and chilli until well pulverised. Remove and place in a large plastic mixing bowl, with beans. Slightly bruise them with a pestle. Add carrots and tomatoes. Bruise them. Add green pawpaw and again, lightly bruise.
2 Add about 4 tablespoons lemon juice with the fish sauce and sugar. Toss with a large spoon. Taste and if necessary, add more chilli, sugar, lemon juice or fish sauce.
3 When satisfied with the flavour and consistency, sprinkle with ground shrimp and toss again. Serve sprinkled with ground peanuts, on a bed of lettuce leaves, with garnishes of your choice.

SERVES 4

PRAWN (SHRIMP) AND ORANGE SALAD

GOONG SOD GUP SOM KEOW WAN

300 g (10 oz) green prawns (shrimps), peeled, deveined, with tails intact
1 tablespoon roasted chilli paste, bought or homemade (see recipe page 29), optional
2 tablespoons lemon juice
1½ tablespoons fish sauce
3 tablespoons water
1 onion, sliced into fine rings
1 teaspoon finely sliced fresh chilli (optional)
4 oranges, peeled, seeded and sliced
1 bunch fresh mint leaves
6 lettuce leaves, to serve

1 Place prawns (shrimps), roasted chilli paste, lemon juice, fish sauce and water in a saucepan. Stir and heat slowly until prawns (shrimps) turn pink. Remove from heat and cool.

2 To prawn (shrimp) mixture, add onion rings, fresh chilli, if using, orange slices and mint leaves. Mix thoroughly.

3 Serve on a bed of lettuce leaves, either chilled or at room temperature, with garnishes of your choice.

SERVES 4

BEEF SALAD WITH CHILLI, ONIONS AND CUCUMBER

YAM NUA

200 g (6½ oz) lean beef, 3 cm (1½ in) thick steaks of fillet or rump

2 tablespoons water

1 tablespoon lemon juice

1 tablespoon fish sauce

1 cucumber, sliced

1 large onion, sliced

1 tablespoon chopped shallots (spring onions)

½ teaspoon fresh or dried chilli (optional)

1 tablespoon chopped fresh coriander leaves

2 tablespoons fresh mint leaves

6 lettuce leaves, to serve

garnishes of your choice

1 Tenderise beef with a mallet if necessary. Barbecue or grill to medium-rare. Cut into fine thin slices about 5 cm x 1 cm (2 in x ½ in). In a saucepan or wok over medium heat braise beef briefly in water, so water absorbs meat flavour. Don't overcook meat.

2 Remove from heat. Add lemon juice, fish sauce, cucumber, onion, shallots, chilli, coriander and mint. Stir together. Arrange on a bed of lettuce leaves. Surround the beef salad with an interesting assortment of colourful garnishes.

SERVES 4

GREEN MANGO SALAD

YAM MAMUANG

Green mangoes aren't always available so this easy-to-make salad can be made with tart green apples instead.

4 green mangoes

2 tablespoons lemon juice

3 to 4 tablespoons dried shrimp, ground finely

2 tablespoons roasted peanuts, ground finely

4 tablespoons fish sauce

2 tablespoons sugar

2 tablespoons roasted chilli paste bought or homemade (see recipe page 29)

¼ cup mint leaves

2 green shallots (spring onions), chopped

4 brown Thai shallots, sliced

¼ cup coriander leaves, chopped

1 small fresh chilli, chopped

6 green salad leaves, to serve

mint and coriander leaves, to garnish

1 Peel, core and slice mangoes into fine shreds. In a bowl, gently combine shredded mango with the lemon juice, dried shrimp, peanuts, fish sauce, sugar and chilli paste.

2 Stir through mint leaves, green shallots (spring onions), brown shallots, coriander leaves and fresh chilli.

3 Taste to see if a little extra sugar or lemon juice is needed to balance flavours.

4 Heap on to a bed of salad leaves and garnish with mint and coriander leaves.

SERVES 4

PRAWN (SHRIMP) SALAD WITH LEMON GRASS AND MINT

YAM PLA GOONG

400 g (13 oz) green prawns (shrimps), shelled, deveined, with tails intact (see Note)

2 tablespoons lemon juice

1½ tablespoons fish sauce

1 tablespoon roasted chilli paste, bought or homemade (see recipe page 29), optional

3 tablespoons water

2 onions, finely sliced in rings

2 tablespoons chopped shallots (spring onions)

2 tablespoons thinly sliced lemon grass

3 tablespoons chopped fresh mint

2 tablespoons chopped fresh coriander leaves

1 teaspoon finely chopped fresh chilli (optional)

4 lettuce leaves, to serve

1 Place prawns (shrimps), lemon juice, fish sauce, roasted chilli paste and water in a saucepan. Stir and heat slowly until prawns (shrimps) turn pink. Taste to see if extra lemon juice or fish sauce is needed.

2 Remove from heat. Add onions, shallots, lemon grass, mint, coriander and fresh chilli, if using. Toss gently. Serve on a bed of lettuce leaves. Garnish as you wish.

Note: This salad is equally, if not more delicious made with lobster tails, tails of Balmain bugs, butterfly lobsters, Moreton Bay bugs, crayfish or any other favourite seafood.

SERVES 4

❖ **CORIANDER**

Coriander is an important ingredient in many Thai recipes. Try growing your own so that you always have a fresh supply.

Coriander is an annual and grows 25 cm to 60 cm (10 in to 24 in) high. It likes full sun. Seeds can be sown at almost any time of the year in moderate climates.

ROSE PETAL AND WATERCRESS SALAD

YAM DOK GULAB

4 tablespoons fish sauce
4 tablespoons lemon juice
2 teaspoons sugar

100 g (3½ oz) cooked chicken, finely sliced
100 g (3½ oz) cooked pork, finely chopped
100 g (3½ oz) cooked prawns (shrimps), chopped (optional)
2 tablespoons ground, roasted, unsalted peanuts
3 cloves garlic, finely chopped, fried golden and drained
2 onions, finely sliced, fried golden and drained
1 bunch watercress, chopped
20 to 30 rose petals, rinsed and drained
6 large lettuce leaves, to serve

GARNISH
fresh mint, chopped
fresh coriander leaves, chopped
chilli strips
chilli flowers
shallot curls

Rose Petal and Watercress Salad. Choose any colour of rose petals and if you like the taste and colour of watercress, add lots more. Choose rose petals from your own garden so that you know they haven't been sprayed.

1 In a bowl, combine fish sauce, lemon juice and sugar. Stir until sugar dissolves.
2 Add chicken, pork, prawns (shrimps) and ground peanuts. Mix well. Add fried garlic and onions and toss lightly.
3 Carefully combine with watercress and most of the rose petals, avoiding bruising the petals.
4 Place in a mound on the lettuce leaves. Garnish with remaining rose petals and other garnish ingredients attractively arranged.

SERVES 4

❖ **CUCUMBERS**

Thai cooking uses lots of cucumber — in soups and salads, and as a garnish. Use any long, green, smooth-skinned cucumber available. They go under a variety of names, depending on what part of the world you live in: English, Lebanese, Cypress or telegraph cucumbers. In most recipes, small round cucumbers, known as apple cucumbers, make an acceptable substitute, but they are not appropriate for stuffing.

CUCUMBER SALAD

YAM THANG KWA

2 cucumbers, peeled, seeded and diced
2 tablespoons finely chopped onion
2 tablespoons sliced shallots (spring onions), cut into 2 cm (¾ in) pieces
2 tablespoons dried shrimp, washed and ground
2 tablespoons finely chopped fresh coriander stems and leaves
4 tablespoons fresh mint leaves
2 tablespoons fish sauce
4 tablespoons lemon juice
1 teaspoon sugar
6 lettuce leaves, to serve

GARNISH
3 tablespoons crushed roasted unsalted peanuts
½ teaspoon dried chilli flakes
mint sprigs
coriander sprigs

1 Drain diced cucumber on absorbent kitchen paper for a few minutes. Combine in a bowl with onion, shallots (spring onions), dried shrimp, chopped coriander and mint leaves.
2 Sprinkle with fish sauce, lemon juice and sugar. Toss gently.
3 Place lettuce leaves on a platter. Arrange cucumber salad in a mound on top. Sprinkle with ground peanuts and dried chilli flakes. Garnish with mint and coriander sprigs.

SERVES 4

SPICY MINCED BEEF

LAAB NUA

Laab Nua, sometimes called Laab Issan, is a Thai version of steak tartare and is thought to have come from the Mongols, or Tartars as they were sometimes called, when the Thai lived in the Yunnan Valley region more than 1000 years ago.

200 g (6½ oz) lean beef, minced or finely chopped
3 tablespoons water
1 tablespoon lemon juice
1 tablespoon fish sauce
1 large onion, finely sliced
1 tablespoon finely chopped shallots (spring onions)
2 tablespoons rice, dry-fried and ground
4 tablespoons fresh mint leaves
1 tablespoon finely chopped fresh coriander stem and leaves
1 tablespoon finely sliced lemon grass
½ teaspoon chilli powder or finely chopped fresh chilli

GARNISH
fresh basil leaves, coriander leaves, mint leaves, shallot curls and chilli flowers, lettuce leaves, snake beans or sliced cucumber (any combination)

In a saucepan, braise beef in water using a wooden spoon to separate, until beef is medium-rare and still quite pink. Remove from heat. Combine beef with lemon juice, fish sauce, onion, shallots (spring onions), ground rice, mint leaves, coriander, lemon grass and chilli powder. Place in a mound on a bed of lettuce leaves and decorate with garnishes of your choice.

SERVES 4

GLASS NOODLE SALAD

YAM WOON SEN

200 g (6½ oz) lean chicken or pork, minced, or 200 g (6½ oz) whole green prawns (shrimps), peeled
3 tablespoons or more chicken Thai Soup Stock (see recipe page 34)
1½ tablespoons lemon juice
1 tablespoon fish sauce
1 tablespoon roasted chilli paste, bought or homemade (see recipe page 29)
100 g (3½ oz) cellophane noodles, soaked in warm water for 10 minutes and drained
1 large onion, sliced
2 tablespoons chopped shallots (spring onions)
2 tablespoons chopped fresh coriander leaves
2 tablespoons fresh mint leaves
6 lettuce leaves or Chinese cabbage leaves, to serve

1 In a saucepan over medium heat, braise meat in stock for several minutes. Add lemon juice, fish sauce and roasted chilli paste. Cook another few minutes.
2 Add half the drained noodles. Toss gently, making sure mixture remains moist. Add remaining noodles and a little more stock if necessary.
3 Taste to see if extra seasoning is required; if you want it more spicy, add a little more roasted chilli paste or some dried or fresh chilli.
4 When satisfied with the flavour and consistency, add onion, shallots, coriander and mint. Toss gently. Serve on a bed of lettuce.

SERVES 4

FRESH WHOLE CORIANDER WITH SPICY TAMARIND DIP

NAM PLA WAN PAK CHEE

This is a dish for lovers of that taste so synonymous with Thai cuisine — fresh coriander. In Thailand, whole coriander plants are often served as a side dish to a meal. Here's a recipe for a traditional sauce that has been popular for generations, one that especially complements fresh coriander, and is served at a meal with barbecued fish or prawns (shrimps). The sauce should be eaten freshly made.

6 whole fresh coriander plants, roots included

3 tablespoons dried shrimp, soaked for 5 minutes and drained

2 large dried chillies, soaked 10 minutes and drained

½ cup (125 ml/4 fl oz) tamarind juice

1 tablespoon fish sauce

2 tablespoons palm or brown sugar

1 Spanish or brown onion, neatly sliced

2 cloves garlic, finely sliced

1 teaspoon chopped fresh coriander leaves

1 Prepare coriander plants by cleaning thoroughly and removing any broken or yellowing leaves (do not remove roots). Arrange on a serving plate and set aside.
2 Dry-fry dried shrimp in a heavy-based frypan for several minutes. Remove from pan and grind or pound finely.
3 Slice chillies finely and dry-fry, seeds included. Mix in a small bowl with tamarind juice, fish sauce and sugar. Stir well. Taste to see if extra tamarind juice, fish sauce or sugar is needed to balance the flavours of hot, sweet, sour and salty.
4 Stir in ground shrimp, onion, garlic and coriander leaves. If necessary, add a little boiled water to thin the sauce.
5 Place in a bowl accompanied by the plate of whole coriander plants. Serve as a green salad side dish. To eat, simply break off a piece of stem or root, and dip in the sauce.

SERVES 4

STIR-FRIED MIXED VEGETABLES

PAD PAK RUAM

3 tablespoons vegetable oil

2 cloves garlic, finely chopped

400 to 500 g (13 oz to 1 lb) mixed vegetables eg Chinese cabbage, broccoli, green beans, brussels sprouts, cucumber, carrots, lettuce, cabbage, Chinese broccoli, bok choy, bean sprouts or spinach (any combination)

3 tablespoons water

1 tablespoon fish sauce

1 tablespoon oyster sauce

½ teaspoon sugar

½ teaspoon white pepper

1 Heat oil in a wok over high heat. Stir-fry garlic for a few seconds. Add vegetables (except bean sprouts, if using).
2 Stir-fry quickly for about 1 minute while vegetables splutter noisily because of their high water content. Add water, fish and oyster sauces, sugar and pepper. Stir quickly and cook for another 1 to 2 minutes, until vegetables are lightly cooked but crisp. If using bean sprouts, stir in just before you finish cooking. Remove from heat and serve.

SERVES 4

good

CRISP DEEP-FRIED VEGETABLES

PAK TOD

A side dish of crisp fried vegetables coated in a feather-light batter.

BATTER (see Note)
125 g (4 oz) cornflour
½ teaspoon salt
1 teaspoon sugar
1 teaspoon baking soda
½ cup (125 ml/4 fl oz) vegetable oil
½ cup (125 ml/4 fl oz) tepid water

VEGETABLES
3 to 4 cups of a variety of fresh vegetables cut in uniform sizes eg broccoli, cauliflower, champignons, carrot, zucchini (courgette), celery, capsicum (pepper), green beans
2 cups (500 ml/16 fl oz) vegetable oil, for deep-frying

1 TO PREPARE BATTER: Place cornflour, salt, sugar, baking soda, oil and some of the water in a bowl. Beat lightly with a fork. Add more water if necessary to achieve a thin batter. Wait for bubbles to appear on the surface. Chill for 30 minutes.
2 Lightly coat vegetable pieces with batter. Deep-fry in very hot oil until just golden. Remove and drain on absorbent kitchen paper. Skim any burnt pieces of batter from the surface of the oil and take care the oil doesn't get too hot and smoke or burn. Serve with a bowl of Sweet Chilli Dipping Sauce (see recipe page 16).
Note: This homemade batter may be replaced with commercial tempura mix, available at supermarkets and delicatessens.

SERVES 4

Stir-fried Mixed Vegetables, Fresh Whole Coriander with Spicy Tamarind Dip, Crisp Deep-fried Vegetables and Sweet Chilli Dipping Sauce.

1 *In a large saucepan, bring vinegar, sugar and salt to the boil and add vegetables.*

2 *Stir-fry the paste.*

3 *Serve warm sprinkled with sesame seeds.*

Pour into sterilised jars. If covered tightly, Pickled Vegetables will keep for 1 to 2 weeks.

Chillies are part of the capsicum (pepper) family. Generally the smaller the chilli the hotter the taste. If you prefer your food slightly milder then cut down the amount of chilli in your recipes. Gradually you will find that your tolerance for the 'hotness' increases.

PICKLED VEGETABLES

PAK DONG

3 cups (750 ml/1¼ pt) white vinegar
1½ tablespoons sugar
2 teaspoons salt
250 g (8 oz) cauliflower pieces
250 g (8 oz) cucumber, peeled, seeded and diced
250 g (8 oz) baby corn
100 g (3½ oz) carrots, sliced
100 g (3½ oz) broccoli, bok choy or Chinese broccoli pieces
200 g (6½ oz) cabbage, cut into pieces
4 cloves garlic, finely chopped
1 onion, finely chopped
6 dried red chillies, seeded and chopped
1 cup (250 ml/8 fl oz) peanut oil
1 tablespoon sesame seeds, dry-fried until golden
fresh coriander leaves, to garnish

1 In a large saucepan, bring vinegar, sugar and salt to the boil. Add all the vegetables except garlic, onion and chillies. Blanch for about 1 minute, ensuring they remain crisp. The leafy vegetables will probably need less cooking time, so use your discretion.
2 Remove from heat. Set aside, leaving vegetables to stand in the vinegar syrup.
3 In a food processor, blend garlic, onion and chillies to a smooth paste. In a wok or large frypan, heat oil and stir-fry paste for several minutes.
4 Add blanched vegetables and their syrup. Stir and cook for about 1 minute, combining flavours but being careful not to break up vegetables or overcook them.
5 Serve warm on a dish sprinkled with roasted sesame seeds and garnished with coriander, or cool and pour into sterilised jars for later use. If covered tightly, jars can be stored for a week or two.

SERVES 4

PICKLED GARLIC

GRATEUM DONG

1 cup (250 ml/8 fl oz) white vinegar
4 cups (1 litre/1¾ pints) water
3 tablespoons sugar
1 tablespoon salt
6 bulbs garlic (about 100 cloves), peeled unless skin is really tender
3 x 300 ml (10 fl oz) screw-top jars, cleaned and sterilised

1 In a saucepan, bring vinegar, water, sugar and salt to the boil. Reduce heat and simmer for about 5 minutes.
2 Add garlic and boil for 1 to 2 minutes. Remove from heat.
3 Cool and pour into sterilised jars. Keeps for months in the refrigerator, but wait at least a week before eating, for the full flavour to develop.

MAKES ABOUT 3 x 300 ML (10 FL OZ) JARS

MIXED VEGETABLES IN COCONUT SAUCE

PAK TOM KATI

1 cup (250 ml/8 fl oz) coconut milk
1 tablespoon fish sauce
2 teaspoons sugar
2 fresh Kaffir lime leaves (or if dried, soaked for 5 minutes in hot water) (optional)
½ teaspoon pepper
½ a small onion, sliced
1 fresh red chilli, finely sliced (optional)
100 g (3½ oz) peas
100 g (3½ oz) sliced green beans
30 g (1 oz) mushrooms, sliced
60 g (2 oz) eggplant (aubergine), thickly sliced
100 g (3½ oz) English spinach, chopped
100 g (3½ oz) Chinese cabbage, shredded

1 In a saucepan, bring coconut milk, fish sauce, sugar, lime leaves and pepper to the boil.
2 Reduce heat. Add onion and simmer for 2 minutes. Taste to see if more sugar or fish sauce is needed.
3 Add vegetables, the leafier ones last. Simmer until the vegetables are just cooked. Serve with rice or noodles.

SERVES 4

PICKLED LEMONS OR LIMES

MANAO DONG

10 small green (unripe) lemons or limes
180 g (6 oz) salt
3 to 4 cups (750 ml to 1 litre/ 1¼ to 1¾ pt) water
1 tablespoon sugar

1 Choose smooth-skinned lemons that are not too young and pithy. Roll each lemon on a flat surface with a plate for several minutes to soften.
2 Rub skin well with dampened salt to coat. Leave overnight. If it's sunny, leave lemons in the sun for a few hours the following day.
3 Boil water, salt and sugar for 5 minutes. Allow to cool. Place lemons in sterilised jars and pour salty water over them. Seal and do not use for at least 3 months. Will keep indefinitely.

MAKES 2 x 300 ML/10 FL OZ JARS

PORK STUFFED OMELETTE

KAI YAD SAI MUU SAB

2 tablespoons vegetable oil
**4 eggs, lightly beaten with
1 tablespoon fish sauce**
**chopped fresh coriander
leaves, to garnish**

FILLING

1 small clove garlic, finely chopped
1 small onion, finely chopped
**2 tablespoons finely chopped
coriander root**
100 g (3½ oz) lean pork, minced
1 tomato, chopped
**60 g (2 oz) snow peas, green beans
or capsicum (pepper),
finely chopped**
1 teaspoon sugar
1 teaspoon pepper
½ tablespoon fish sauce

1 TO PREPARE FILLING: Heat half
the oil in a wok or frypan. Stir-fry
garlic until golden, Add onion and
coriander root. Stir-fry for another
minute. Add minced pork and stir-
fry until brown.
2 Add tomato and green
vegetables. Cook for several
minutes. Season with sugar, pepper
and fish sauce. Taste for flavour,
then remove from heat.
3 TO PREPARE THE OMELETTE: In
an omelette pan or frypan, heat
remaining tablespoon of oil over
medium heat. Pour in egg and fish
sauce mixture. When omelette
begins to set, put pork and
vegetable mixture in the centre.
Fold sides of omelette over to form
a square. When omelette is golden
underneath, turn it over like a
pancake and brown on the other side.
4 Can be served as a square, or
sliced into serving portions. If
individual omelettes are preferred,
simply cook in smaller quantities.
Garnish with chopped coriander
leaves.

SERVES 4

STIR-FRIED ASPARAGUS

PAD NAW MAI FARANG

2 tablespoons vegetable oil
2 cloves garlic, finely chopped
**400 g (12½ oz) fresh asparagus,
sliced into 5 cm (2 in) pieces**
2 tablespoons oyster sauce
1 tablespoon fish sauce
1 teaspoon white pepper
1 teaspoon sugar

1 Heat oil in a wok or frypan.
Stir-fry garlic until golden. Add
asparagus and stir-fry for 1 minute.
Stir in oyster and fish sauces, pepper
and sugar.
2 Taste and add extra seasoning,
if needed. Stir-fry for another 1 to
2 minutes. Remove from heat and
serve.

SERVES 4

Stir-fried Asparagus.

SALTED EGGS

KAI KEM

375 g (12 oz) salt
**8 to 10 cups (2 to 2.5 litres/3½ to
4½ pt) water**
12 whole fresh eggs in their shells

1 Bring salt and water to the boil.
Remove from heat and cool until
lukewarm.
2 Place eggs carefully in a large
glass or earthenware jar. Pour the
brine over them until eggs are
completely covered. Seal the jar and
stand in a cool place for at least
1 month.
3 Boil or fry before serving.

MAKES 12

1 *Make filling in a wok then remove from heat.*

2 *Cook omelette in an omelette pan or frypan.*

3 *When omelette begins to set, add filling and fold over.*

Pork Stuffed Omelette.

DESSERTS
AND
THAI
SWEETS

The Thai fondness for sweets is apparent everywhere in Thailand. And it's hard to escape the street vendors, even if you're travelling by train. When the train stops at a station they offer snacks to you through the window and you pray the train will hurry up and move, to help you resist temptation.

Just when you're regretting your willpower and the train is click-clacking along the tracks, the smiling face of the very vendor you've just seen at the station is peering down at you.

He's decided to join the train for a station or two and sell his goodies. And there goes your willpower, straight out the window!

In this chapter we've concentrated on the easiest desserts using local fruits and ingredients.

There are creamy coconut custards and ice creams, fruits in sweet syrups and 'kanoms' or Thai cakes, like coconut squares. But after a sumptuous Thai banquet it's really difficult to go past a platter of assorted fresh fruit (ponlamai).

Mangoes with Sticky Rice (page 90) garnished with thick coconut cream and roasted sesame seeds, and Mango Ice Cream (page 91) garnished with a mint sprig.

1 *Prepare pumpkin by scooping out pulp and seeds. Rinse well and pat dry.*

2 *Pour custard mix into pumpkin and cover with pumpkin lid.*

3 *Steam pumpkin for 30 to 40 minutes. Test with a skewer.*

Steamed Whole Pumpkin with Coconut Custard, chilled and cut into wedges.

STEAMED WHOLE PUMPKIN WITH COCONUT CUSTARD

SANGKAYA FAK TONG

1.5 kg (3 lb) pumpkin, with good colour and shape (see *Note*)

8 eggs, beaten

1 cup (250 ml/8 fl oz) thick coconut milk

125 g (4 oz) sugar, caster or brown

1 Neatly cut off the pumpkin top with stem and retain for a lid. Try not to make the opening too big. Scoop out pulp and seeds, leaving a thick layer of pumpkin meat. Rinse out well and pat dry thoroughly.

2 In a large mixing bowl, beat together eggs, coconut milk and sugar. Pour into pumpkin and cover with its 'lid'.

3 Gently place pumpkin in a large steamer. Cook for 30 to 45 minutes until custard is firm and pumpkin tender. Test with a skewer. Cool, remove and chill overnight. Cut into thick wedges and serve.

Note: If using a large, tough pumpkin you may have to steam it upside down in a steamer for 10 minutes first, cool, pat dry, then fill with custard and steam again another 30 minutes or so.

SERVES 6

THAI FRIED BANANAS

GLUAY TOD

4 large firm bananas, peeled
40 g (1½ oz) butter
100 g (3½ oz) brown sugar
4 tablespoons lemon or lime juice

1 Slice bananas lengthways. Cut in half to make four equal pieces.
2 Heat butter in a wok over medium heat. Fry bananas on both sides until golden. Add sugar. Stir gently until sugar dissolves and turns into a syrup.
3 Remove from heat to a serving bowl. Sprinkle with lemon juice and serve.

SERVES 4

ORANGES IN ROSE OR JASMINE SYRUP

SOM NAMCHUAM

750 g (1½ lb) sugar
1 cup (250 ml/8 fl oz) water
15 to 20 jasmine flowers and few drops jasmine essence or 15 to 20 rose petals and 1 teaspoon rosewater
3 to 4 large oranges or mandarins (tangerines) divided into segments, with pith removed

1 In a large saucepan, combine sugar and water. Bring to the boil. Simmer for 10 minutes until sugar dissolves and a syrup forms. If necessary, strain syrup through cheesecloth. Cool, then add either jasmine essence or rosewater.
2 Place orange or mandarin segments in a large serving bowl. Pour syrup over them. Garnish with jasmine or rose petals and serve immediately.

SERVES 4

BANANAS IN COCONUT SAUCE

GLUAY BUAT CHEE

6 large bananas, peeled
1½ cups (375 ml/12 fl oz) coconut milk
1½ tablespoons sugar
pinch salt

1 Slice bananas diagonally in 2 cm (¾ in) slices.
2 Heat coconut milk in a saucepan. Add sugar and salt. Bring to the boil. Simmer, stirring, for 2 minutes.
3 Remove from heat. Stir in banana slices. Return to the boil for 10 seconds. Remove from heat. Serve with ice cream or Sticky Rice (see recipe page 26).

SERVES 4 TO 6

COCONUT ICE CREAM

ICE CREAM KATI

1¼ cups (300 ml/10 fl oz) thick coconut milk
1½ cups (375 ml/12 fl oz) fresh cream
4 eggs, with 2 yolks separated
1 teaspoon vanilla or rosewater (optional)
125 g (4 oz) sugar
½ teaspoon salt

GARNISH
50 g (2 oz) shredded coconut (sweetened), dry-fried until golden
mint sprigs

1 In a saucepan, heat coconut milk and cream over medium heat, so they cook for several minutes without boiling.
2 In a bowl, beat together 2 eggs and 2 extra yolks, vanilla, sugar and salt. Pour into a double-boiler over boiling water.
3 Gradually beat in warm coconut milk mixture, a few tablespoons at a time. Stir until mixture thickens to coat the back of a spoon. Remove from heat and cool, stirring occasionally.
4 Pour into a metal ice cream tray. Put in the coldest part of the freezer until half frozen, about 1 hour.
5 Scoop into a food processor or chilled bowl and beat thoroughly until smooth. Pour into metal tray again and freeze completely.
6 Serve in scoops, garnished with shredded coconut and mint sprigs.

SERVES 4

CUSTARD SQUARES

KANOM MO KAENG

2 cups (500 ml/16 fl oz) thick coconut milk
7 eggs, beaten
125 g (4 oz) sugar, preferably brown
1 tablespoon rose water (optional)
2 tablespoons desiccated or shredded coconut

1 Preheat oven to 180°C (350°F). Grease a shallow rectangular or square baking dish (about 15 cm/6 in square).
2 Beat together all ingredients in a large bowl.
3 In a double boiler or large bowl set on top of a steamer, stir mixture over boiling water until it thickens to the consistency of soft scrambled eggs.
4 Pour into the baking dish and bake for 30 minutes.
5 Remove and place under a griller on medium heat. Grill until top of custard is golden. It takes only a few minutes so be careful it doesn't burn.
6 Remove, cool and chill, then cut into 4 cm (1¾ in) squares.

SERVES 4 TO 6

Coconut Custard steamed and served garnished in individual bowls. You may eat the jasmine if you're feeling adventurous. Don't eat the banana leaf triangles.

MANGOES WITH STICKY RICE
MAMUANG KHAO NIEO

This is one of the most famous Thai 'desserts', eaten as a snack day and night in Thailand. It's sold wrapped in a banana leaf from roadside vendors and also adorns the menus of some of the most expensive Bangkok restaurants. It's the perfect finale to a Thai feast and will have your guests begging for more.

**375 g (12 oz) freshly cooked
Sticky Rice (see recipe page 26)
1 cup (250 ml/8 fl oz) thick
coconut milk
4 tablespoons sugar
2 teaspoons salt
4 tablespoons coconut cream,
skimmed from top of coconut milk
roasted sesame seeds, to garnish
6 large ripe mangoes, peeled,
halved, stoned**

1 Make sticky rice according to recipe. Place in a bowl and set aside.
2 In a saucepan over medium heat, bring coconut milk, sugar and salt to the boil. Lower heat and simmer until milk thickens, about 4 to 5 minutes.
3 Pour mixture carefully over sticky rice. Fluff up rice with a fork, allowing coconut mixture to trickle through but not 'drown' the rice (otherwise it becomes too gluggy and you lose the lovely translucent quality of the sticky rice).
4 Allow rice to stand for 10 minutes. Turn out in a mound on a serving platter. Garnish with thick coconut cream sprinkled with sesame seeds.
5 Slice mangoes and arrange around the mound of sticky rice. Alternatively, make individual servings of sticky rice and mango slices.

SERVES 4 TO 6

1 *Strain custard through muslin or cheesecloth, so the mixture is fine and smooth.*

2 *Steam until firm.*

COCONUT CUSTARD
SANGKAYA

**1 cup (250 ml/8 fl oz) thick
coconut milk
4 eggs, beaten
125 g (4 oz) sugar**

1 Beat coconut milk, eggs and sugar together until sugar dissolves and mixture is well blended.
2 Sieve through muslin or cheesecloth so mixture is fine and smooth.
3 Place in a serving bowl inside a steamer. Steam until firm. Alternatively, you can steam the custard in individual serving bowls.

SERVES 4

Tropical Fruits in Jasmine Syrup. If you don't have an elaborately carved watermelon on hand, use a large clear glass bowl.

MANGO ICE CREAM

ICE CREAM MAMUANG

4 ripe mangoes or 400 to 500 g (13 oz to 1 lb) canned sliced mango
180 g (16 oz) sugar, (125 g/4 oz) if using canned mango
1 tablespoon lemon juice
1 tablespoon gelatine, dissolved in 3 tablespoons water
1½ cups (375 ml/12 fl oz) thickened cream, whipped until stiff
extra mango slices
fresh mint sprigs, to garnish

1 Peel, seed and cut mangoes. Place in a bowl with sugar, lemon juice and dissolved gelatine. Mix well until sugar dissolves. Fold in whipped cream.
2 Spoon into a metal tray. Place in the coldest part of the freezer until half frozen.
3 Remove and place in a food processor or chilled bowl. Beat until smooth.

4 Return to freezer tray. Freeze completely. Serve with fresh sliced ripe mango, garnished with mint sprigs.

SERVES 4

TROPICAL FRUITS IN JASMINE OR LIME SYRUP

PONLAMAI NAMCHUAM

This simple syrup with a combination of tropical fruits of your choice can make a stunning dessert, especially if served in a hollowed out, decorated watermelon or other smooth-skinned melon. If you don't have the time, simply serve in an attractive glass bowl.

2 cups (500 ml/16 fl oz) water
500 g (1 lb) sugar
few drops jasmine essence or teaspoon of lime or lemon zest
1 small rockmelon, scooped into balls
1 small honeydew melon, scooped into balls
1 small pawpaw, scooped into balls
1 small pineapple, diced
assorted cherries, lychees, seedless grapes or other favourite fruit
fresh mint leaves, to garnish

1 In a saucepan, bring water, sugar and jasmine essence to the boil. Cook for 10 minutes to form a syrup.
2 Taste to see whether extra jasmine essence is required. If the syrup is not completely clear, cool and strain through cheesecloth.
3 Arrange fruits in a serving bowl. Pour enough syrup over to cover them. Chill and serve. Alternatively, pour syrup over the fruit, chill, then spoon into a hollowed, chilled melon. Garnish with mint leaves.

SERVES 6 TO 8

BANQUETS AND MENUS

A typical Thai meal consists of rice and at least five other dishes. There's usually a soup, a fried dish, a curry, something steamed or braised, and a salad of cooked or raw vegetables. Dessert is often a simple platter of assorted fresh fruit.

If you want to have a traditional Thai dinner, you can sit on the floor, serve everything at once and eat with forks and spoons. Today, however, most urban Thai families eat Western style. If you really want to get serious about traditional Thai, you should try to have a few hot sauces on hand. The Thais serve at least one and sometimes several at a meal. They're a bit like the spicy, hot sambals of Java and Bali. Some varieties are commercially available, but the best are homemade.

In this section, we've selected a range of meals but you'll have to adjust the recipes occasionally to suit the number of diners. Most recipes have 200 to 300 g (6½ to 10 oz) of the main ingredient (eg meat, seafood, vegetable) so you can expect four to six people to get a reasonable taste of each dish. Most of the meals are intended to be shared by four people, but each meal is generally equivalent to one main course.

Read every recipe carefully and make your own judgment about how hungry your guests are likely to be, then plan and adjust accordingly.

THAI BANQUET TRADITIONAL

FOR 8 TO 10 PEOPLE

Savoury Seafood Rolls (Hae Guen)
Sweet Pork (Muu Wan)
snack-sized pieces
Hot and Sour Chilli Sauce
(Nam Prik Keega)
Sweet and Sour Cucumber Relish
(Thang Kwa Preow Wan)
Stir-fried Ginger Chicken
(Pad King Gai)
Salted Fish (Pla Kem)
Chilli Prawns (Shrimps)
(Goong Pad Prik)
Muslim Beef Curry
(Gaeng Mussaman Nua)
Flaked Fish with Tamarind Sauce
(Nam Prik Tha Dang)
Steamed Rice (Khao Plow)
Stuffed Cucumber Soup
(Gaeng Chud Thang Kwa Sod Sai)
Cucumber Salad (Yam Thang Kwa)
Duck Casserole (Tom Kem Ped)
Assorted Fresh Fruit (Ponlamai)
(choose any seasonal fruit you like)

SEAFOOD BANQUET

FOR 6 TO 8 PEOPLE

Spicy Deep-fried Fish Cakes
(Tod Man Pla)
Sweet and Sour Cucumber Relish
(Thang Kwa Preow Wan)
Prawn (Shrimp) and Pork Toast
(Kanom Pang Muu Goong)
Spicy Prawn (Shrimp) Soup
(Tom Yam Goong)
Stir-fried Seafood with Fresh Herbs
(Ahahn Talay)
Whole Fish with Ginger Sauce

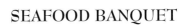
(Pla Jian)
Spicy Mussels with Chilli and Lime
Leaves (Gaeng Choo Chee
Hoi Mang Pu)
Prawn (Shrimp) Salad with Lemon Grass
and Mint (Yam Pla Goong)
Carrot and Green Bean Salad with
Pawpaw (Som Tam)
Steamed Rice (Khao Plow)
Bananas in Coconut Sauce
(Gluay Buat Chee)

THAI STYLE DINNER

FOR 6 TO 8 PEOPLE

Spicy Deep-fried Fish Cakes
(Tod Man Pla)
Sweet and Sour Cucumber Relish
(Thang Kwa Preow Wan)
Crisp Deep-fried Vegetables (Pak Tod)
Sweet Chilli Dipping Sauce
(Nam Jim Wan)
Spicy Chicken, Coconut and Galangal
Soup (Tom Kah Gai)
Red Pork Curry (Gaeng Ped Muu)
Beef with Basil, Chilli and Green Beans
(Nua Pad Krapao)
Prawns (Shrimps) with Garlic and
Pepper served with Greens
(Goong Tod Grateum)
Calamari (Squid) Salad with Mint,
Onion and Lemon Grass
(Yam Pla Meuk)
Carrot and Green Bean Salad with
Pawpaw (Som Tam)
Steamed Rice (Khao Plow)
Bananas in Coconut Sauce
(Gluay Buat Chee)

TRADITIONAL THAI DINNER

FOR 6 TO 8 PEOPLE

Roast or Barbecued Pork with Somi's
Spicy Dipping Sauce
(Muu Yahng)
Duck Steamed with Chinese Melon and
Pickled Limes (Ped Thoon Manao Dong)
Chiang Mai Noodles
(Khao Soi Chiang Mai)
Salted Fish (Pla Kem)
Assorted Raw Vegetable Pieces with
Spicy Dried Shrimp Sauce
(Nam Prik Kapi)
Panang Beef Balls (Panang Nua)
Chilli Fish Sauce (Nam Pla Prik)
Steamed Rice (Khao Plow)
Assorted Fresh Fruit (Ponlamai)
(choose any seasonal fruit you like)

SEAFOOD DINNER

FOR 4 TO 6 PEOPLE

Spicy Deep-fried Fish Cakes
(Tod Man Pla)
Sweet and Sour Cucumber Relish
(Thang Kwa Preow Wan)
Vegetable and Prawn (Shrimp) Soup
(Gaeng Liang)
Spicy Mussels with Chilli and Lime
Leaves (Gaeng Choo Chee Hoi Mang Pu)
Whole Fish with Fresh Chilli, Garlic
and Coriander (Pla Lad Prik)
Prawn (Shrimp) Salad with Lemon Grass
and Mint (Yam Pla Goong)
Green Mango Salad (Yam Mamuang)
Steamed Rice (Khao Plow)
Steamed Whole Pumpkin with Coconut
Custard (Sangkaya Fak Tong)

EASY THAI DINNER

FOR 4 TO 6 PEOPLE

Steamed Mussels with Lime Leaves and
Galangal (Hoi Mang Pu Ob Mordin)
Spicy Chicken, Coconut and
Galangal Soup (Tom Kah Gai)
Chilli Beef (Nua Pad Prik)
Prawns (Shrimps) with Garlic and
Pepper served with Greens
(Goong Tod Grateum)
Red Pork Curry (Gaeng Ped Muu)
Steamed Rice (Khao Plow)
Assorted Fresh Fruit (Ponlamai)
(choose any seasonal fruit you like)

MILDLY SPICED THAI MEAL

FOR 4 TO 6 PEOPLE

Crisp Fried Calamari (Squid)
(Pla Meuk Tod)
Sweet Chilli Dipping Sauce
(Nam Jim Wan)
Stir-fried Beef with Broccoli (Pak Pad
Gup Nua)
Vegetable and Prawn (Shrimp) Soup
(Gaeng Liang)
Chicken Salad with Mint, Onion and
Lemon Grass (Laab Gai)
Mixed Vegetables in Coconut Sauce
(Pak Tom Kati)
Simple Fried Rice (Khao Pad Tamada)
Thai Fried Bananas (Gluay Tod)

INDEX

MEASURING MADE EASY

HOW TO MEASURE DRY INGREDIENTS

15 g	½ oz	
30 g	1 oz	
60 g	2 oz	
90 g	3 oz	
125 g	4 oz	(¼ lb)
155 g	5 oz	
185 g	6 oz	
220 g	7 oz	
250 g	8 oz	(½ lb)
280 g	9 oz	
315 g	10 oz	
345 g	11 oz	
375 g	12 oz	(¾ lb)
410 g	13 oz	
440 g	14 oz	
470 g	15 oz	
500 g	16 oz	(1 lb)
750 g	24 oz	(1½ lb)
1 kg	32 oz	(2 lb)

QUICK CONVERSIONS

5 mm	¼ inch	
1 cm	½ inch	
2 cm	¾ inch	
2.5 cm	1 inch	
5 cm	2 inches	
6 cm	2½ inches	
8 cm	3 inches	
10 cm	4 inches	
12 cm	5 inches	
15 cm	6 inches	
18 cm	7 inches	
20 cm	8 inches	
23 cm	9 inches	
25 cm	10 inches	
28 cm	11 inches	
30 cm	12 inches	(1 foot)
46 cm	18 inches	
50 cm	20 inches	
61 cm	24 inches	(2 feet)
77 cm	30 inches	

NOTE: We developed the recipes in this book in Australia where the tablespoon measure is 20 ml. In many other countries the tablespoon is 15 ml. For most recipes this difference will not be noticeable.

However, for recipes using baking powder, gelatine, bicarbonate of soda, small amounts of flour and cornflour, we suggest you add an extra teaspoon for each tablespoon specified.

Many people find it very convenient to use cup measurements. You can buy special measuring cups or measure water in an ordinary household cup to check it holds 250 ml (8 fl oz). This can then be used for both liquid and dry cup measurements.

MEASURING LIQUIDS

METRIC CUPS

¼ cup	60 ml	2 fluid ounces
⅓ cup	80 ml	2½ fluid ounces
½ cup	125 ml	4 fluid ounces
¾ cup	180 ml	6 fluid ounces
1 cup	250 ml	8 fluid ounces

METRIC SPOONS

¼ teaspoon	1.25 ml
½ teaspoon	2.5 ml
1 teaspoon	5 ml
1 tablespoon	20 ml

OVEN TEMPERATURES

TEMPERATURES	CELSIUS (°C)	FAHRENHEIT (°F)	GAS MARK
Very Slow	120	250	½
Slow	150	300	2
Moderate	160-180	325-350	3-4
Moderately hot	190-200	375-400	5-6
Hot	220-230	425-450	7-8
Very hot	250-260	475-500	9-10

Published by Murdoch Books®, a division of Murdoch Magazines Pty Limited, 213 Miller Street, North Sydney NSW 2060.

Photographer: Ashley Barber
Food Stylists: Georgina Dolling, Michelle Gorry
The publishers would like to thank the following for their help in the photography for this book: Home and Garden on the Mall, Sydney; Studio-Haus, Double Bay. Fabrics supplies by Carol Selvarajah.

Murdoch Books® Associate Food Editors: Kerrie Ray, Tracy Rutherford. Publisher: Anne Wilson. Publishing Manager: Catie Ziller. Production Coordinator: Liz Fitzgerald. Managing Editor: Susan Tomnay. Creative Director: Marylouise Brammer. International Manager: Mark Newman. Marketing Manager: Mark Smith. National Sales Manager: Karon McGrath. Photo Librarian: Dianne Bedford.

National Library of Australia Cataloguing-in-Publication Data: Miller, Somi Anuntra. Thai cooking class. Rev. ed. Includes index. ISBN 0 86411 514 8. 1. Cookery, Thai. I. Lake, Patricia. II. Title. (Series: Bay Books cookery collection.) 641.59593. First published in Australia in 1989. This edition 1996. Printed by Griffin Press, Adelaide.